KNOWING SCRIPTURE

R.C. Sproul

foreword by
J.I. Packer

InterVarsity Press
Downers Grove
Illinois 60515

InterVarsity Press
P.O. Box 1400, Downers Grove, IL 60515-1426
World Wide Web: www.ivpress.com
E-mail: mail@ivpress.com

InterVarsity Press® is the book-publishing division of InterVarsity Christian Fellowship/USA®, a student movement active on campus at hundreds of universities, colleges and schools of nursing in the United States of America, and a member movement of the International Fellowship of Evangelical Students. For information about local and regional activities, write Public Relations Dept., InterVarsity Christian Fellowship/USA, 6400 Schroeder Rd., P.O. Box 7895, Madison, WI 53707-7895, or visit the IVCF website at <www.ivcf.org>.

Scripture quotations, unless otherwise noted, are from the Revised Standard Version of the Bible, *copyright 1946, 1952, 1971 by the Division of Christian Education of the National Council of the Churches of Christ in the U.S.A., and are used by permission.*

ISBN 0-87784-733-9

Library of Congress Catalog Card Number 77-011364

Printed in the United States of America ∞

P	44	43	42	41	40	39	38	37	36
Y	12	13	11	10	09	08	07	06	

To my father,
Robert C. Sproul, Jr.,
a layman who loved the Book

1

Why Study the Bible

Two Myths——————————————————————13
The Clarity of Scripture ——————————————15
The Problem of Motivation ————————————17
The Biblical Basis for Bible Study ————————19
The Bible as Revelation———————————————23
Theory and Practice ———————————————————25
The Sensuous Christian————————————————27
A Matter of Duty——————————————————————30

2

Personal Bible Study & Private Interpretation

Martin Luther and Private Interpretation ————33
Objectivity and Subjectivity——————————————37
The Role of the Teacher—————————————————40

3

Hermeneutics: The Science of Interpretation

The Analogy of Faith————————————————————46
Interpreting the Bible Literally ————————————48
Literal Interpretation and Genre Analysis ————49
The Problem of Metaphor—————————————————53
The Medieval Quadriga——————————————————54
The Grammatico-Historical Method ——————————56
Source Criticism ——————————————————————57
Authorship and Dating ——————————————————58
Grammatical Errors ————————————————————60

4

Practical Rules for Biblical Interpretation

Rule 1. Like Any Book —————————————————63
Rule 2. Reading Existentially—————————————65
Rule 3. The Historical and the Didactic ——————68
Rule 4. The Implicit and the Explicit ——————————75
Rule 5. The Meaning of Words ————————————79
Rule 6. Parallelism —————————————————85
Rule 7. Proverb and Law ——————————————89
Rule 8. The Spirit and the Letter ——————————90
Rule 9. Parables—————————————————94
Rule 10. Predictive Prophecy ————————————97

5

Culture & the Bible

Cultural Conditioning and the Bible ————————101
Cultural Conditioning and the Reader ——————104
Principle and Custom ————————————————106
Practical Guidelines—————————————————108

6

Practical Tools for Bible Study

Bible Translations——————————————————113
Annotated Bibles ——————————————————115
The King James Bible————————————————116
Commentaries ———————————————————118
Concordances, Bible Dictionaries and Atlases ——119
Foreign Translations ————————————————120
Bible Reading Program for Beginners———————120
What about Greek and Hebrew? ——————————123
Conclusion ————————————————————125

FOREWORD

If I were the devil (please, no comment), one of my first aims would be to stop folk from digging into the Bible. Knowing that it is the Word of God, teaching men to know and love and serve the God of the Word, I should do all I could to surround it with the spiritual equivalent of pits, thorn hedges and man traps, to frighten people off. With smug conceit, no doubt, as if receiving a compliment, I should acknowledge that wise old Jonathan Edwards had me absolutely taped when he wrote: "The devil never would attempt to beget in persons a regard to that divine word which God has given to be the great and standing rule.... Would the spirit of error, in order to deceive men, beget in them a high opinion of the infallible rule, and incline them to think much of it, and be very conversant with it? ... The devil has ever shown a mortal spite and hatred towards that holy book the Bible: he has done all in his power to extinguish that light.... He is engaged against the Bible, and hates every word in it." I should labor every day to prove Edwards's words true.

How? Well, I should try to distract all clergy from preaching and teaching the Bible, and spread the feeling that to study this ancient book directly is a burdensome extra which modern Christians can forgo without loss. I should broadcast doubts about the truth and relevance and good sense and straightforwardness of the Bible, and if any still insisted on reading it I should lure them into assuming that the benefit of the practice lies in the noble and tranquil feelings evoked by it rather than in noting what Scripture actually says. At all costs I should want to keep them from using their minds in a disciplined way to get the measure of its message.

Were I the devil, taking stock today, I think I might be pleased at the progress I had made. But I should be very far from pleased to see this book by my friend—sorry, J. I. Packer's friend—"R. C."

For more than a century, Protestant theology has been in conflict about the Bible. The first storm center was inspiration and its corollary, inerrancy. Fifty years ago, the debate shifted to revelation, the method and content of God's communication through allegedly fallible Scriptures. Interpretation is now the central interest, and the subjectivism which yesterday concluded that the Bible is neither true nor trustworthy today interprets it on the basis that its message to us is neither consistent nor clear. The results of so doing are often muddled and messy. Against this background, Dr. Sproul's vigorous layman's introduction to the interpretive task is more than welcome.

What are its special qualities? Clarity, common sense, mastery of material and a bubbling enthusiasm which turns the author from a good communicator into a superb one. The Bible excites him and his excitement is infectious. O taste and see! Sproul on Bible study will make you want to study the Bible, as well as equipping you to do so: and what greater virtue could such a book have than that? There are technical problems in hermeneutics that lie beyond its scope, but the basics are here, with a most salutary stress on the objectivity (the "there-ness") of God's instruction in the Scriptures and on the rationality of the method of deciphering and applying it. It is a pleasure and a privilege to commend to the Christian public a book calculated to do so much good.

J. I. Packer
Trinity College
Bristol, England

PREFACE

The last twenty years have seen a renewal of interest in the Scriptures. Since neo-orthodox theology called the church back to a serious study of the content of the Bible, there has been more concern in the life of the church for understanding and applying its message to our generation. Along with this new interest, however, has come confusion; there has been little agreement among Christian scholars concerning the rudimentary principles of biblical interpretation. This confusion in the scholarly world has made an impact on the life of the whole church.

Our day seems to be the age of "lay renewal." Much of this renewal is associated with home Bible studies and small group fellowships. Many people now gather to discuss, debate and comment on the Scripture for themselves. Often they find themselves disagreeing about what the Bible means or how it should be applied. This has had unfortunate consequences.

For many, the Bible remains an enigma capable of vastly different interpretations. Some have even given over to despair about their own ability to make sense of it. To others the Bible has a nose of wax capable of being shaped into conformity with the vested interests of the reader. Too often the conclusion seems to be, "You can quote the Bible to prove anything."

Is there any way out of this confusion? Can serious readers find any principles to guide them through the conflicting viewpoints they hear from all sides? These are some of the questions that this book is designed to deal with.

Although many of the issues have a scholarly dimension, I have not been motivated by a desire to enter the academic debate concerning the science of hermeneutics. Rather my prime motivation is to offer basic, "common sense" guidelines to help serious readers study sacred Scripture profitably. In line with the Bible's own view of itself, the book seeks to emphasize the divine origin and authority of Scripture. Because of this, I have attempted to provide rules of interpretation that will serve as a check and balance for our all-too-common tendency to interpret the Bible according to our own prejudices. The book closes with a survey of various tools that are available to help either beginners or more advanced students of the Bible.

Above all, I would like this to be a practical book that will give assistance to lay people. Indeed, I have a fond hope that Christians will continue their study of the Scripture and continue the contributions they are making in the church. May this book be an encouragement to persevere with joy as well as understanding.

I owe a debt of gratitude to a number of people who assisted me in this project. My special thanks go to Mary Semach for typing the manuscript. And I also wish to acknowledge the help of Stuart Boehmig, who assisted in making necessary revisions, and to Prof. David Wells, whose advice has been invaluable in correcting the manuscript.

R. C. Sproul
The Ligonier Valley

1

Why Study the Bible?

Why study the Bible? It may seem odd and foolish to raise this question since you probably would not be reading this book unless you were already convinced that Bible study is necessary. Our best intentions, however, are often weakened by our moods and caprice. Bible study often falls by the way. So, before we examine the practical guidelines for Bible study, let us review some of the compelling reasons for studying the Bible at all.

Two Myths
First, we will look at some of the reasons people give for not studying the Bible. These "reasons" often contain myths which are passed off as truisms through much repetition. The myth that claims first place in our hall of excuses is the idea that the Bible is too difficult for the ordinary person to understand.

Myth 1: The Bible is so difficult to understand that only highly skilled theologians with technical training can deal with the Scriptures.

This myth has been repeated many times by sincere

people. People say, "I know I can't study the Bible, because every time I try to read it, I can't understand it." When some people say that, they may want to hear, "That's all right. I understand. It's really a difficult book, and unless you've had seminary training, maybe you ought not to tackle it." Or perhaps they want to hear, "I know, it's too heavy, too deep, too profound. I commend you for your tireless efforts, your strenuous labors in trying to solve the mystifying riddle of God's Word. It is sad that God has chosen to speak to us in such obscure and esoteric language that only scholars can grasp it." This, I am afraid, is what many of us want to hear. We feel guilty and want to quiet our consciences for neglecting our duty as Christians.

When we express this myth, we do it with astonishing ease. The myth is so often repeated that we do not expect it to be challenged. Yet we know that as mature adults, living in the United States of America, having a high-school education or better, we can understand the basic message of the Bible.

If we can read the newspaper, we can read the Bible. In fact, I would venture to guess that more difficult words and concepts are expressed on the front page of a newspaper than on most pages of the Bible.

Myth 2: The Bible is boring.

If we press people for an explanation for what they mean when they express the first myth, usually they respond by saying, "Well, I guess I can understand it, but frankly the book bores me to death." This statement reflects not so much an inability to understand what is read as a taste and preference for what one finds interesting and exciting.

The preponderance of boredom that people experience with the Bible came home to me several years ago when I was hired to teach the Scriptures in required Bible courses at a Christian college. The president of the institution phoned me and said, "We need someone young and exciting, someone with a dynamic method who will be able to 'make the Bible come alive.'" I had to force myself to swallow my words. I wanted to say, "You want me to make the Bible come alive? I didn't know that it had died. In fact, I never even heard that it was ill. Who was the attending physician at the Bible's demise?" No, I can't make the Bible come alive for anyone. The Bible is already alive. It makes me come alive.

When people say the Bible is dull it makes me wonder why. Biblical characters are full of life. There is a unique quality of passion about them. Their lives reveal drama, pathos, lust, crime, devotion and every conceivable aspect of human existence. There is rebuke, remorse, contrition, consolation, practical wisdom, philosophical reflection and, most of all, truth. Perhaps the dullness some experience is due to the antiquity of the material that may seem foreign. How does the life of Abraham—lived so long ago and so far away—relate to us? But the characters of biblical history are real. Though their life settings are different from ours, their struggles and concerns are very much like ours.

The Clarity of Scripture
In the sixteenth century, the Reformers declared their total confidence in what they called the perspicuity of Scripture. What they meant by that technical term was the *clarity* of Scripture. They maintained that the Bible is basically clear and lucid. It is simple enough for any literate person to understand its *basic message*. This is not to say that all parts of the Bible are equally clear or that there are no difficult passages or sections to be found in it. Laymen unskilled in the ancient languages and the fine points of exegesis may have difficulty with parts of Scripture, but the essential content is clear enough to be understood easily. Luther, for example, was convinced that what was obscure and difficult in one part of Scripture was stated more clearly and simply in other parts of Scripture.

Some parts of the Bible are so clear and simple that they are offensive to those suffering from intellectual arrogance. A few years ago I was lecturing about how Christ's death on the cross fulfilled the curse motif of the Old Testament. In the middle of my lecture a man in the audience interrupted me, saying loudly, "That's primitive and obscene." I asked him to repeat his comment so that everyone present could have the opportunity to hear his complaint. When he repeated it, I said, "You are exactly right. I particularly like your choice of words, *primitive* and *obscene*." The entire history of redemption is communicated in primitive terms from the episode of the encounter of Adam and Eve with the serpent to the devastating destruction that God visits on the chariots of Egypt in the Exodus to the crass and brutal murder of Jesus of Nazareth. The Bible reveals a God who hears the groans of all of his people, from the peasant to the philosopher, from the dull-witted to the sophisticated scholar. His message is simple enough for the most simplistic of his fallen creatures to understand. What kind of a God would reveal his love and redemption in terms so technical and concepts so profound that only an elite corps of professional scholars could understand them? God does speak in primitive terms because he is addressing himself to primitives. At the same time, there is enough profundity contained in Scripture to keep the most astute and erudite scholars busily engaged in their theological inquiries for a lifetime.

If *primitive* is an appropriate word to describe the content of Scripture, *obscene* is even more so. All of the obscenities of sin are recorded with clear and forthright language in the Scripture. And what is more obscene than the cross? Here we have obscenity on a cosmic scale. On the cross Christ takes upon himself human obscenities to redeem them.

If you have been one of those who have clung to the myths of dullness or difficulty, perhaps it is because you have attributed to the whole of Scripture what you have found in some of its parts. Maybe some passages have been peculiarly difficult and obscure. Other passages may have left you bewildered and baffled. Perhaps those should be left for the scholars to unravel. If you find certain portions of the Scripture difficult and complex, need you insist that the whole of Scripture is boring and dull?

Biblical Christianity is not an esoteric religion. Its content is not concealed in vague symbols that require some sort of special "insight" to grasp. There is no special intellectual prowess or pneumatic gift that is necessary to understand the basic message of Scripture. You may find that in Eastern religions where insight is limited to some remote guru who lives in a shanty high in the Himalayas. Maybe the guru has been thunderstruck by the gods with some profound mystery of the universe. You travel to inquire and he tells you in a hushed whisper that the meaning of life is "one-hand clapping." That's esoteric. That's so esoteric that even the guru does not understand it. He cannot understand it because it's an absurdity. Absurdities often sound profound because they are incapable of being understood. When we hear things we do not understand, sometimes we think they are simply too deep or weighty for us to grasp when in fact they are merely unintelligible statements like "one-hand clapping." The Bible does not talk like that. The Bible speaks of God in meaningful patterns of speech. Some of those patterns may be more difficult than others, but they are not meant to be nonsense statements that only a guru can fathom.

The Problem of Motivation

It is important to note that the theme of this book is not how to *read* the Bible but how to *study* the Bible. There is a great deal of difference between reading and studying. Reading is something we can do in a leisurely way, something that can be done strictly for entertainment in a casual, cavalier manner. But study suggests labor, serious and diligent work.

Here then, is the real problem of our negligence. We fail in our duty to study God's Word not so much because it is difficult to understand, not so much because it is dull and boring, but because it is work. Our problem is not a lack of intelligence or a lack of passion. Our problem is that we are lazy.

Karl Barth, the famous Swiss theologian once wrote that all human sin finds its roots in three basic human problems. He included in his list of rudimentary sins, the sins of pride (*hubris*), dishonesty, and slothfulness. None of these basic evils is instantly eradicated by spiritual regeneration. As Christians we must struggle against these problems through our entire pilgrimage. None of us is immune. If we are going to deal with the discipline of Bible study, we must recognize at the outset that we will need the grace of God to persevere.

The problem of slothfulness has been with us since the curse of the Fall. Our labor is now mixed with sweat. Weeds are easier to grow than grass. Newspapers are easier to read than the Bible is to study. The curse of labor is not magically removed simply because it is the study of Scripture that is our task.

I frequently lecture to groups on the theme of studying the Bible. Usually I ask the group how many of them have been Christians for one year or more. Then I ask those people how many have read the entire Bible from cover to cover. In every instance, the overwhelming majority answer in the negative. I would venture to guess that among those who have been Christians for a year or more, at least eighty per cent have never read the whole Bible. How is that possible? Only an appeal to the radical Fall of the human race could begin to answer that question.

If you have read the whole Bible, you are in a small minority of Christian people. If you have studied the Bible, you are in an even smaller minority. Isn't it amazing that almost every American has an opinion to offer about the Bible, and yet so few have really studied it? Sometimes it seems as though the only people who take the time to study it are those with the sharpest axes to grind against it. Many people study it to find possible loopholes so they can get out from under the weight of its authority.

Biblical ignorance is not limited to lay people by any means. I have sat on church boards responsible for the preparation and examination of seminarians preparing for the pastoral ministry. The degree of biblical ignorance manifested by many of these students is appalling. Seminary curricula have not done much to alleviate the problem.

Many churches are ordaining men every year who are virtually ignorant of the content of Scripture.

I was shocked when I took a test in biblical knowledge for entrance to the theological seminary from which I graduated. After I completed my exam, I was deeply embarrassed, ashamed to hand in my paper. I had taken several courses in college that I thought would prepare me for such a test, but when the test came I was not ready. I left question after question blank and was certain that I had failed. When the grades were posted, I discovered that I had received one of the highest grades in a group of seventy-five students. Even with the grades scaled there were several students who scored less than 10 out of a possible grade of 100. My score was poor, yet it was one of the best of the bad.

Biblical illiteracy among the clergy has become so prevalent that we often find pastors getting annoyed and angry when their parishioners ask them to teach them the Bible. In many cases the pastor lives in mortal fear that his ignorance will be exposed by his being thrust into a situation where he is expected to teach the Bible.

The Biblical Basis for Bible Study

The Bible itself has much to say about the importance of studying the Bible. Let us examine two passages, one from each testament, in order to catch a glimpse of these mandates.

In Deuteronomy 6 we find a passage that was familiar to every Jew of the Old Testament. Its words were used to call the assembly together for worship. We read: "Hear, O Israel! The LORD is our God, the LORD is one! And you shall love the LORD your God with all your heart and with all your soul and with all your might" (vv. 4-5). Most of us are familiar with these words. But what follows them immediately? Read on:

> *And these words, which I am commanding you today, shall be on your heart; and you shall teach them diligently to your sons and shall talk of them when you sit in your house and when you walk by the way and when you lie*

down and when you rise up. And you shall bind them
as a sign on your hand and they shall be as frontals on
your forehead. And you shall write them on the doorposts
of your house and on your gates. (vv. 6-9)
Here God sovereignly commands that his Word be taught so
diligently that it penetrates the heart. The content of that
Word is not to be mentioned casually and infrequently. Repeated discussion is the order of the day, every day. The call
to bind on the hand, the forehead, the doorpost and gate
makes it clear that God is saying that the job must be done
by whatever method it takes.

Looking at the New Testament we read Paul's admonition
to Timothy:

You, however, continue in the things you
have learned and become convinced of,
knowing from whom you have learned
them; *and that from childhood you have*
known the sacred writings which are
able to give you the wisdom that leads
to salvation through faith which is in
Christ Jesus. All Scripture is inspired
by God and profitable for teaching, for
reproof, for correction, for training in
righteousness; that the man of God may be
adequate, equipped for every good work.
(2 Tim. 3:14-17)

This exhortation is so basic to our understanding of the importance of Bible study that it warrants a careful scrutiny.

Continue in the things you have learned. This part of the
admonition lays the accent on *continuity.* Our study of Scripture is not to be a once-for-all matter. There is no room for
the proverbial once over lightly. Consistency is necessary for
a sound basis of biblical studies.

Sacred writings which are able to give you the wisdom that
leads to salvation. Paul refers to the Scripture's ability to
give wisdom. When the Bible speaks of "wisdom," it refers
to a special kind of wisdom. The term is not used to connote
an ability to be "worldly-wise" or to have the cleverness

necessary to write a *Poor Richard's Almanac*. In biblical terms, wisdom has to do with the practical matter of learning how to live a life that is pleasing to God. A cursory glance at the Wisdom Literature of the Old Testament makes this emphasis abundantly clear. Proverbs, for example, tells us that wisdom begins with the "fear of the LORD" (Prov. 1: 7; 9:10). That fear is not a servile fear but a posture of awe and reverence which is necessary for authentic godliness. The Old Testament distinguishes between wisdom and knowledge. We are commanded to acquire knowledge, but more to acquire wisdom. Knowledge is necessary if wisdom is to be gained, but it is not identical with wisdom. One can have knowledge without having wisdom, but one cannot have wisdom without having knowledge. A person without knowledge is ignorant. A person without wisdom is deemed a fool. In biblical terms foolishness is a moral matter and receives the judgment of God. Wisdom in the highest sense, is being wise with respect to salvation. Thus wisdom is a theological matter. Paul is saying that through the Scriptures we can acquire that kind of wisdom that concerns our ultimate fulfillment and destiny as human beings.

Knowing from whom you have learned them. Who is this "whom" Paul is talking about? Is he referring to Timothy's grandmother? Or to Paul himself? These options are doubtful. The "whom" refers to the ultimate source of the knowledge Timothy has acquired, namely, God. This comes out more clearly in the statement, "All Scripture is inspired by God."

Scripture inspired by God. This passage has been the focal point of volumes of theological literature that describe and analyze theories of biblical inspiration. The crucial word in the passage is the Greek term *theopneust* which is often translated by the phrase "inspired by God." The term more precisely means "God-breathed," which refers not so much to God's breathing something "in" as to his breathing something "out." Rather than the term "inspiration," we may be better advised to render the Greek by the English "expiration." In that case we would see the significance of the passage not so much in providing us with a theory of inspiration—a theory of how God transmitted his Word through human authors—but rather a statement of the origin or source of Scripture. What Paul is saying to Timothy is that the Bible comes from God. He is its ultimate author. It is his word; it comes from him; it carries the weight of all that he is. Thus, the injunction to remember "from whom you have learned them [these things]."

Scripture is profitable for teaching. One of the most important priorities Paul mentions is the pre-eminent way in which the Bible profits us. The first and indeed foremost profit is the profit of teaching or instruction. We may pick up the Bible and be "inspired" or moved to tears or other poignant emotions. But our greatest profit is in being *instructed*. Again, our instruction is not in matters of how to build a house or how to multiply and divide or how to employ the science of differential equations; rather we are instructed in the things of God. This instruction is called "profitable" because God himself places an extremely high value on it. The instruction is assigned worth and significance.

Countless times I have heard Christians say, "Why do I need to study doctrine or theology when all I need to know is Jesus?" My immediate reply is this: "Who is Jesus?" As soon as we begin to answer that question, we are involved in doctrine and theology. No Christian can avoid theology. Every Christian is a theologian. Perhaps not a theologian in the technical or professional sense, but a theologian nevertheless. The issue for Christians is not whether we are going to be theologians but whether we are going to be good theologians or bad ones. A good theologian is one who is *instructed* by God.

Scripture profitable for reproof, correction, and training in righteousness. In these words Paul articulates the practical value of Bible study. As fallen creatures we sin, we err and we are inherently out of shape with respect to righteousness. When we sin, we need to be reproved. When we err, we need to be corrected. When we are out of shape, we need to go into training. The Scriptures function as our chief reprover, our chief corrector and our chief trainer. The bookstores of this world are filled with books on training methods to acquire excellence in sports, to lose weight and get our physical figures into shape and to acquire skills in all areas. Libraries have stacks of books written to teach us financial management and the nuances of wise investment policies. We can find many books that will teach us how to turn our losses into profits, our liabilities into assets. But where are the books that will train us in righteousness? The question still remains, "What shall it profit a man if he wins the whole world and loses his soul?"

That the man of God may be adequate, equipped for every good work. The Christian who is not diligently involved in a serious study of Scripture is simply inadequate as a disciple of Christ. To be an adequate Christian and competent in the things of God one must do more than attend "sharing sessions" and "bless-me parties." We cannot learn competency by osmosis. The biblically illiterate Christian is not only inadequate but unequipped. In fact, he is inadequate because he is not equipped. Lee Trevino may be able to put on incredible exhibitions of his prodigious skill by hitting golf balls with a taped up Dr. Pepper bottle. But he doesn't use a Dr. Pepper bottle off the tee in the U. S. Open.

The Bible as Revelation
One of the most important advantages the Bible gives us is that it provides information that is not available anywhere else. Our universities provide us with a wealth of knowledge acquired by human investigation of the natural world. We learn by observation, analysis and abstract speculation. We compare and contrast varied opinions from notable scholars. But with all the skills of knowledge that we have at our disposal in this world, there is no one who can speak to us from a transcendent perspective, no one who can reason with us, as the philosophers say, *sub species aeternitatis.*

Only God can provide us with an eternal perspective and speak to us with absolute and final authority. The advantage of the equipment provided by Scripture is that knowledge is made available to us that can be learned from no other source. The Scripture does, of course, talk of matters that can be learned by other means. We are not utterly dependent on the New Testament to learn who Caesar Augustus was or how far it is from Jerusalem to Bethany. But the world's best geographer cannot show us the way to God, and the world's best psychiatrist cannot give us a final answer to the problem of our guilt. There are matters contained in Holy Writ that "unveil" for us that which is not exposed to the natural course of human investigation.

Though much can be learned about God from a study of nature, it is his self-revelation in Scripture that is most complete and most valuable for us. There is an analogy between how we get to know people in this world and how we become acquainted with God. If we want to learn something about a human being, let's say Bill Monroe, there are many ways we can go about it. We might write to the F.B.I. or the C.I.A. and find out if they have a file on him. We could send for his high-school and college transcripts. Through such records we might discover his basic biographical history, medical record, academic and athletic achievement records. We could then interview his friends to get a more personal evaluation. But all these methods are indirect, and many of Bill's intangible qualities will remain obscured to our scrutiny. All these methods are but secondary sources of information.

If we want more accurate knowledge of Bill Monroe, we should meet him personally, observe his outward appearance, see how he behaves, what mannerisms he employs. We may even be able to guess how he is feeling, what he is thinking, what he values, and what displeases him. But if we want to gain intimate knowledge of him we have to engage in some kind of verbal communication with him. No one can express more clearly or more accurately what he believes, feels or thinks than the person himself. Unless Bill chooses to reveal those things verbally, our knowledge will be limited to guesswork and speculation. Only words will enlighten us.

Likewise, when we speak about the concept of revelation, we are talking about the basic principle of self-disclosure. The Scriptures come to us as divine self-disclosure. Here the mind of God is laid bare on many matters. With a knowledge of Scripture we do not have to rely on secondhand information or bare speculation to learn who God is and what he values. In the Bible he reveals himself.

Theory and Practice

Like the Christian who shuns theology, there are those who despise any kind of quest for theoretical knowledge of God, insisting instead on being "practical." The spirit of America has been defined as the spirit of pragmatism. This spirit is manifested nowhere more clearly than in the arena of politics and in the public school system which has been informed by the principles and methods of education set down by John Dewey.

Pragmatism may be defined simply as the approach to reality that defines truth as "that which works." The pragmatist is concerned about results and the results determine the truth. The problem with this kind of thinking, if left uninformed by the eternal perspective, is that the results tend to be judged in terms of short-range goals.

I experienced this dilemma when my daughter enrolled in the public school system by way of kindergarten. She attended a very progressive school outside of Boston. After a few weeks we received notification from the school that the principal was holding an open meeting for parents in order to explain the program and procedures employed in the kindergarten. At the meeting the principal carefully explained the daily schedule. He said, "Don't be alarmed if your child comes home and tells you that he was playing with puzzles or modeling clay in school. I can assure you that everything in the daily routine is done with a purpose. From 9:00 A.M. to 9:17 A.M. the children play with puzzles that are carefully designed by orthopedic experts and are designed to develop the motor muscles of the last three fingers of the left hand."

He went on to explain how every minute of the child's day was planned with skilled precision to insure that everything was done with a purpose. I was duly impressed.

At the end of his presentation the principal asked for questions. I raised my hand and said, "I am deeply impressed by the careful planning that has gone into this program. I can see that everything is done with a purpose in view. My question is, How do you decide which 'purposes' to employ? What final purpose do you use to decide the individual purposes? What is the overall purpose of your purposes? In other words, what kind of a child are you trying to produce?"

The man turned white and then scarlet, and in stumbling terms he replied, "I don't know; no one ever asked me that question." I appreciated the candor of his reply and the genuine humility it displayed, yet at the same time, his answer terrified me. How can we have purposes without purpose? Where can we go to discover the ultimate test for our pragmatism? Here is where transcendent revelation is most critical to our lives. Here is where the content of Scripture is most relevant for our practice. God alone can give us the final evaluation of the wisdom and value of our practices.

The person who despises theory and calls himself practical is not wise. The person who concerns himself only with short-term goals may have big trouble when it comes to the very long run of eternity. It must also be added that there is no practice without some underlying theory. We do what we do because we have a theory about the value of doing it. Nothing betrays our deepest theories more eloquently than our practice. We may never think seriously about our theories or subject them to rigorous critical analysis, but we all have them. As in the case of the Christian who wants Christ without theology, so the person who wants practice without theory will usually wind up with bad theories that will lead to bad practice.

Because the theories found in Scripture proceed from God, the Bible is eminently practical. Nothing could be more practical than God's Word because it proceeds from a theory that is established from the eternal perspective. The fatal weakness of pragmatism is overcome by revelation.

The Sensuous Christian

I often have been tempted to write a book by the title *The Sensuous Christian*. *The Sensuous Woman, The Sensuous Man, The Sensuous Couple, The Sensuous Divorcee,* ad nauseam, all have become best sellers. Why not *The Sensuous Christian?*

What is a sensuous Christian? One dictionary defines *sensuous* as, "pertaining to the senses or sensible objects: highly susceptible to influence through the senses." The sensuous Christian is one who lives by his feelings rather than through his understanding of the Word of God. The sensuous Christian cannot be moved to service, prayer or study unless he "feels like it." His Christian life is only as effective as the intensity of present feelings. When he experiences spiritual euphoria, he is a whirlwind of Godly activity; when he is depressed, he is a spiritual incompetent. He constantly seeks new and fresh spiritual experiences and uses them to determine the Word of God. His "inner feelings" become the ultimate test of truth.

The sensuous Christian doesn't need to study the Word of God because he already knows the will of God by his feelings. He doesn't want to know God; he wants to experience him. The sensuous Christian equates "childlike faith" with ignorance. He thinks that when the Bible calls us to childlike faith it means a faith without content, a faith without understanding. He doesn't know that the Bible says, "In evil be babes, but in your thinking be mature" (1 Cor. 14:20). He doesn't realize that Paul tells us again and again, "My beloved brethren, I would not have you ignorant" (see, for example, Rom. 11:25).

The sensuous Christian goes his merry way until he encounters the pain of life that is not so merry and he folds. He usually ends up embracing a kind of "relational theology" (that most dreadful curse on modern Christianity) where personal relationships and experience take precedence over the Word of God. If the Scripture calls us to action that may jeopardize a personal relationship, then the Scripture must be compromised. The highest law of the sensuous Christian is that bad feelings must be avoided at all cost.

The Bible is addressed *primarily* though not *exclusively* to our understanding. That means the mind. This is difficult to communicate to modern Christians who are living in what may be the most anti-intellectual period of Western civilization. Notice, I did not say anti-academic or anti-technological or anti-scholarly. I said anti-intellectual. There is a strong current of antipathy to the function of the mind in the Christian life.

To be sure, there are historical reasons for this kind of reaction. Many laymen have felt the result of what one theologian has called "the treason of the intellectual." So much skepticism, cynicism and negative criticism have spewed forth from the intellectual world of theologians that the laymen have lost their *trust* in intellectual enterprises. In many cases there is the fear that faith will not hold up under intellectual scrutiny so the defense becomes the denigration of the human mind. We turn to feelings rather than to our minds to establish and preserve our faith. This is a very serious problem we face in the twentieth-century church.

Christianity is supremely intellectual though not intellectualistic. That is, Scripture is addressed to the intellect without at the same time embracing a spirit of intellectualism. The Christian life is not to be a life of bare conjecture or cold rationalism; it is to be a life of vibrant passion. Strong feelings of joy, love and exaltation are called for again and again. But those passionate feelings are a *response* to what we understand with our minds to be true. When we read in Scripture, "Take courage; I have overcome the world" (Jn. 16:33), "ho hum" is not an appropriate response. We can be of good cheer because we understand that Christ has indeed overcome the world. That thrills our souls and sets our feet to dancing. What is more precious than to experience the sweetness of the presence of Christ or the nearness of the Holy Spirit?

God forbid that we should lose our passion or go through

the Christian pilgrimage without any experience of Christ. But what happens when there is a conflict between what God says and what I feel? We must do what God says, like it or not. That is what Christianity is all about.

Reflect for a moment. What happens in your own life when you act according to what you feel like doing rather than what you know and understand God says you should do? Here we encounter the ruthless reality of the difference between happiness and pleasure. How easy it is to confuse the two! The pursuit of happiness is regarded as our "unalienable right." But happiness and pleasure are not the same thing. Both of them feel good, but only one endures. Sin can bring pleasure, but never happiness. If sin were not so pleasurable, it would hardly represent a temptation. Yet, while sin often "feels good," it does not produce happiness. If we do not know the difference, or worse yet, do not care about the difference, we have made great strides to becoming the ultimate sensuous Christian.

It is precisely at the point of discerning the difference between pleasure and happiness that knowledge of Scripture is so vital. There is a remarkable relationship between God's will and human happiness. The fundamental deception of Satan is the lie that obedience can never bring happiness. From the primordial temptation of Adam and Eve to last night's satanic seduction, the lie has been the same. "If you do what God says, you will not be happy. If you do what I say, you will be 'liberated' and know happiness."

What would have to be true for Satan's argument to be true? It would seem that for Satan's argument to be true, God would have to be one of three things: ignorant, malevolent or deceptive. It could be that God's Word will not work for us because it proceeds from his divine blunderings. God simply doesn't know enough to tell us what we need to do to achieve happiness. Perhaps he desires our well-being, but simply does not know enough to instruct us properly. He would like to help us out, but the complexities of human life and human situations just boggle his mind.

Perhaps God is infinitely wise and knows what is good for

us better than we do. Perhaps he does understand the complexities of man better than the philosophers, moralists, politicians, school teachers, pastors and the American Psychiatric Society, but he hates us. He knows the truth but leads us astray so he can remain the only happy being in the cosmos. Perhaps his law is an expression of his desire to take gleeful delight in our misery. Thus his malevolence toward us leads him to the role of Great Deceiver. Nonsense! If that were true, then the only conclusion we could come to is that God is the Devil and the Devil is God and Holy Scripture is really the manual of Satan.

Absurd? Unthinkable? I wish it were. In literally thousands of pastors' studies, people are being counseled to act against Scripture because the pastor wants them to be happy. "Yes, Mrs. Jones, go ahead and divorce your husband despite the fact that you are without biblical warrant, for I am sure you will never find happiness married to a man like that."

If there is a secret, a carefully guarded secret, to human happiness, it is that one expressed in a seventeenth-century catechism that says, "Man's chief end is to glorify God and to enjoy him forever." The secret to happiness is found in obedience to God. How can we be happy if we are not obedient? How can we be obedient if we do not know what it is we are to obey? Thus, the top and the tail of it is that happiness cannot be fully discovered as long as we remain ignorant of God's Word.

To be sure, knowledge of God's Word does not guarantee that we will do what it says, but at least we will know what we are supposed to be doing in our quest for human fulfillment. The issue of faith is not so much whether we believe in God, but whether we believe the God we believe in.

A Matter of Duty

Why should we study the Bible? We have mentioned briefly the practical value, the ethical importance and the way of happiness. We have looked at some of the myths that are given why people do not study the Bible. We have examined something of the spirit of pragmatism and the anti-intellectual climate of our day. There are many facets to the question and countless reasons why we ought to study the Bible.

I could plead with you to study the Bible for personal edification; I could try the art of persuasion to stimulate your quest for happiness. I could say that the study of the Bible would probably be the most fulfilling and rewarding educational experience of your life. I could cite numerous reasons why you would benefit from a serious study of Scripture. But ultimately the main reason why we should study the Bible is because it is our duty.

If the Bible were the most boring book in the world, dull, uninteresting and seemingly irrelevant, it would still be our duty to study it. If its literary style were awkward and confusing, the duty would remain. We live as human beings under an obligation by divine mandate to study diligently God's Word. He is our Sovereign, it is his Word and he commands that we study it. A duty is not an option. If you have not yet begun to respond to that duty, then you need to ask God to forgive you and to resolve to do your duty from this day forth.

2

Personal Bible Study & Private Interpretation

It is tacitly assumed that every home in America has a Bible. The Bible remains the perennial best seller in this country. Perhaps many of them serve merely as decorations or as a convenient place to store photos and press flowers, handy also to display in a prominent place when the pastor is visiting the home. Because of the easy accessibility of Bibles, it is easy for us to forget the awesome price that was paid for the privilege of possessing a Bible written in our own language which we can interpret for ourselves.

Martin Luther and Private Interpretation
Two of the great legacies of the Reformation were the principle of private interpretation and the translation of the Bible into the vernacular. The two principles go hand in hand and were accomplished only after great controversy and persecution. Scores of persons paid with their lives by being burned at the stake (particularly in England) for daring to translate the Bible into the vernacular. One of

Luther's greatest achievements was the translation of the Bible into German so that any literate person could read it for himself.

It was Luther himself who brought the issue of private interpretation of the Bible into sharp focus in the sixteenth century. Hidden beneath the famous response of the Reformer to the ecclesiastical and imperial authorities at the Diet of Worms was the implicit principle of private interpretation.

When asked to recant of his writings, Luther replied, "Unless I am convinced by Sacred Scripture or by evident reason, I cannot recant. For my conscience is held captive by the Word of God and to act against conscience is neither right nor safe. Here I stand, I can do no other, God help me." Notice that Luther said "unless I am convinced. . . ." In earlier debates at Leipzig and Augsburg, Luther had dared to presume to interpret Scripture contrary to interpretations rendered both by Popes and by church councils. That he would be so presumptuous led to the repeated charge of arrogance by church officials. Luther did not take those charges lightly but agonized over them. He believed that he could be wrong but maintained that the Pope and councils could also err. For him only one source of truth was free from error. He said, "The Scriptures never err." Thus, unless the leaders of the church could convince him of his error, he felt duty-bound to follow what his own conscience was convinced Scripture taught. With this controversy the principle of private interpretation was born and baptized with fire.

After Luther's bold declaration and subsequent work of translating the Bible into German at Wartburg, the Roman Catholic Church did not roll over and play dead. The church mobilized its forces into a three-pronged counteroffensive known as the Counter Reformation. One of the sharpest prongs of the counterattack was the formulations against Protestantism made by the Council of Trent. Trent spoke to many of the issues raised by Luther and other Reformers. Among those issues was the issue of private interpretation. Trent said:

To check unbridled spirits it [the Council] decrees that no one, relying on his own judgment shall in matters of faith and morals pertaining to the edification of Christian doctrine, distorting the Holy Scriptures in accordance with his own conceptions presume to interpret them contrary to that sense which Holy Mother Church to whom it belongs to judge of their true sense and interpretation has held or holds or even contrary to the unanimous teaching of the Fathers, even though such interpretations should never at any time be published.

Do you catch the flavor of this pronouncement? The statement is saying, among other things, that it is the responsibility of the teaching office of the Roman Catholic Church to expound the Scriptures and to declare the meaning of the Scriptures. This is not to be a matter of private judgment or private opinion. This statement by Trent was clearly designed to speak to the Reformation principle of private interpretation.

If we examine the statement closely, however, we can see that it contains a very serious misunderstanding of the Reformed principle. Did the Reformers promote the notion of unbridledness? Does private interpretation mean that an individual has the right to interpret Scripture to suit himself? May a person interpret Scripture in a whimsical, capricious manner with no restraint? Should the private individual take seriously the interpretations of others such as those who specialize in teaching the Scriptures? The answers to these questions are obvious. The Reformers were also concerned with ways and means to check unbridled spirits. (That is one of the reasons they worked so hard to delineate sound principles of biblical interpretation as a check and balance to fanciful interpretation.) But the way in which they sought to check unbridled spirits was not to declare the teachings of churchmen infallible.

Perhaps the most crucial term that appears in Trent's declaration is the word *distorting*. Trent says that no one has the private right to distort the Scriptures. With that, the Reformers most heartily agreed. Private interpretation never meant that individuals have the right to distort the Scriptures. With the right of private interpretation comes the sober responsibility of accurate interpretation. Private interpretation gives license to interpret but not to distort.

When we look back to the Reformation period and see the brutal response of the Inquisition and the persecutions of those who translated the Scriptures into the vernacular to make them available for laymen, we are horrified. We wonder how the princes of the Roman Catholic Church could be so corrupt as to torture people for reading the Bible. It staggers our imagination even to read of such things. What is often overlooked in such historical reflection, however, is that there were many well-meaning people involved in that action. Rome was convinced that, if you put the Bible into the hands of unskilled laymen and left them to interpret the Book, grotesque distortions would emerge and these would lead the sheep astray, perhaps into everlasting torment. Thus, to protect the sheep from embarking upon a course of ultimate self-destruction, the Church resorted to corporal punishment, even to the point of execution.

Luther was aware of the dangers of such a move but was convinced of the clarity of Scripture. Thus, though the dangers of distortion were great, he thought that the benefit of exposing multitudes to the basically clear message of the gospel would bring far more to ultimate salvation than to ultimate ruin. He was willing to take the risk to turn the valve that might open a "floodgate of iniquity."

Private interpretation opened the Bible for laymen, but it did not do away with the principle of the educated clergy. Going back to biblical days, the Reformers recognized that in Old and New Testament practice and teaching there was a significant place for the rabbi, the scribe and the ministry of teaching. That teachers should be skilled in the ancient languages, customs, history and literary analysis is still an important feature of the Christian church. Luther's famous doctrine of the "priesthood of all believers" has been frequently misunderstood. It does not mean that there is no distinction between clergy and laity. The doctrine simply maintains that every individual Christian has a role to perform and a function to maintain in the total ministry of the church. We are all called to be "Christ to our neighbor" in a certain sense. But that does not mean that the church has no overseers or teachers.

Many people have become disenchanted with the organized church in our present culture. Some have over-reacted in the direction of ecclesiastical anarchy. Out of the cultural revolution of the 60s with the advent of the Jesus movement and the underground church came the cry of the young people, "I don't have to go to anybody for a pastor; I don't believe in an organized church or a structured government of the body of Christ." In the hands of such people the principle of private interpretation could be a license for radical subjectivism.

Objectivity and Subjectivity

The great danger of private interpretation is the clear and present danger of subjectivism in biblical interpretation. The danger is more widespread than is often immediately apparent. I see it manifested very subtly in the course of theological discussion and debate.

Recently I participated in a panel with biblical scholars. We were discussing the pros and cons of a particular passage of the New Testament whose meaning and application were in dispute. In his opening statement, one of the New Testament scholars said, "I think that we should be open and honest about how we approach the New Testament. In the final analysis we all read what we want to read in it, and that's all right." I could not believe my ears. I was so stunned, I offered no rebuttal. My shock was mixed with a sense of futility at the possibility of having a significant exchange of ideas. It is rare to have a scholar state his prejudice so forthrightly in public. We all may struggle with the sinful tendency to read into Scripture what we want to find, but I hope that we do not always do that. I trust there are means available to us to check that tendency.

On the popular level this easy acceptance of the spirit of

subjectivism in biblical interpretation is equally prevalent. Many times after discussing the meaning of a passage, people rebut my statements by simply saying to me, "Well, that's your opinion." What could such a remark mean? First, it is perfectly obvious to all present that an interpretation that I have offered as my own is *my* opinion. I am the one who just gave the opinion. But I don't think that is what people have in mind.

A second possible meaning is that the remark indicates an unspoken rebuttal employing the guilt by association fallacy. By pointing out that the opinion offered is mine, perhaps the person feels that is all that is necessary to rebut it since everybody knows the unspoken assumption: any opinion that comes from the mouth of R. C. Sproul must be wrong because he never has been and never could be right. However hostile people may be to my opinions, I doubt that that is what they mean when they say, "That's your opinion."

I think the third alternative is what most people mean: "That's your interpretation, and that's fine for you. I don't agree with it, but my interpretation is equally valid. Though our interpretations are contrary and contradictory, they can both be true. Whatever you like is true for you and whatever I like is true for me." This is subjectivism.

Subjectivism and subjectivity are not the same things. To say that truth has a subjective element is one thing; to say that it is utterly subjective is quite another. For truth or falsehood to have any significance for my life it must be applied in some way to me. The statement, "It is raining in Georgia" may in fact be true objectively but have no relevance to my life. I may be made to see that it does have relevance if, for example, it could be shown that along with the rain there is also severe hail that is destroying the crop of peaches in which I have just invested my money. Then the statement takes on subjective relevance to me. When the truth of a proposition hits home to me and grasps me, that is a subjective matter. The application of a biblical text to my life may have strong subjective overtones. But that is not what we mean by subjectivism. Subjectivism takes place when we distort the objective meaning of terms to suit our own interests. To say, "It is raining in Georgia," may have no relevance to my life in Pennsylvania, but the words are still meaningful. It means something to the people in Georgia, if not to the plants and the animals that live there. Subjectivism takes place when the truth of a statement is not merely expanded or applied to the subject, but when it is absolutely determined by the subject. If we are to avoid distortion of Scripture, we must avoid subjectivism from the beginning.

In seeking an objective understanding of Scripture, we do not thereby reduce Scripture to something cold, abstract and lifeless. What we are doing is seeking to understand what the word says in its context *before* we go about the equally necessary task of applying it to ourselves. A particular statement may have numerous possible personal applications, but it can only have one correct meaning. Alternate interpretations which are contradictory and mutually exclusive cannot both be true unless God speaks with a forked tongue. We will treat this matter of contradiction and the singular meaning of statements in the Bible more fully later. Presently, however, we are concerned with setting forth the goals of sound biblical interpretation. The first such goal is to arrive at the objective meaning of Scripture and to avoid the pitfalls of distortion caused by letting interpretations be governed by subjectivism.

Biblical scholars make a necessary distinction between what they call *exegesis* and *eisogesis*. *Exegesis* means to explain what Scripture says. The word comes from the Greek word meaning, "to guide out of." The key to exegesis is found in the prefix "ex" which means "from" or "out of." To exegete Scripture is to get out of the words the meaning that is there, no more and no less. On the other hand, *eisogesis* has the same root but a different prefix. The prefix *eis,* also coming from the Greek, means "into." Thus, eisogesis involves reading into the text something that isn't there at all. Exegesis is an objective enterprise. Eisogesis involves an exercise in subjectivism.

All of us have to struggle with the problem of subjectivism. The Bible often says things we do not want to hear. We can put earmuffs on our ears and blinders on our eyes. It is much easier and far less painful to criticize the Bible than to allow the Bible to criticize us. No wonder Jesus frequently concluded his words by saying, "He who has ears to hear, let him hear" (e.g., Luke 8:8; 14:35).

Subjectivism not only produces error and distortion, but it breeds arrogance as well. To believe what I believe simply because I believe it or to argue that my opinion is true simply because it is *my* opinion is the epitome of arrogance. If my views cannot stand the test of objective analysis and verification, humility demands that I abandon them. But the subjectivist has the arrogance to maintain his position with no objective support or corroboration. To say to someone, "If you like to believe what you want to believe, that's fine; I'll believe what I want to believe," only sounds humble on the surface.

Private views must be evaluated in light of outside evidence and opinion because we bring excess baggage to the Bible. No one on the face of this Earth has a perfectly pure understanding of Scripture. We all hold some views and entertain some ideas that are not of God. Perhaps if we knew precisely which of our views were contrary to God, we would abandon them. But to sort them out is very difficult. Thus, our views need the sounding boards and honing steel of other people's research and expertise.

The Role of the Teacher

In the Reformed churches of the sixteenth century a distinction was made between two kinds of elders: teaching elders and ruling elders. Ruling elders were called to govern and administer the affairs of the congregation. Teaching elders, or pastors, were responsible primarily for teaching and equipping the saints for ministry.

The last decade or so has been a remarkable time of church renewal in many places. Para-ministry organizations such as Faith at Work have done much to restore the significance of the laity for the local church. Lay renewal conferences are commonplace. The accent is no longer so much on great pulpiteers but on great programs for and by lay people. This is the era not of the great preacher, but the era of the great congregation.

One of the most significant developments of the lay renewal movement has been the advent of small home Bible study groups. Here, in an atmosphere of congeniality and informality, people who otherwise would not be interested in the Bible have made great strides in learning it. The small group dynamic is basically one that keys on laymen. Laymen teach each other or pool their own ideas in these Bible studies. Such groups have been quite successful in renewing the church. They will be even more so as the people acquire better and better skills in understanding and interpreting the Bible. It is a tremendous thing that people are beginning to open up the Bible and study it together. But it is also an exceedingly dangerous thing. Pooling of knowledge is edifying to the church; pooling of ignorance is destructive and can manifest the problem of the blind leading the blind.

Though small groups and home Bible studies can be very effective in promoting renewal of the church and the transformation of society, somewhere along the line people must receive educated teaching. I am convinced that now, as much as ever, the church needs an educated clergy. Private study and interpretation must be balanced by the collective wisdom of the teachers. Please do not misunderstand. I am not calling the church to return to the pre-Reformation situation where the Bible was held captive by the clergy. I am rejoicing that people are starting to study the Bible on their own and that the blood of the Protestant martyrs was not shed in vain. What I am saying is that it is wise for laymen involved in Bible study to do it in connection with or under the authority of their pastors or professors. It is Christ himself who has ordered his church so as to endow some with the gift of teaching. That gift and that office must be respected if Christ is to be honored by his people.

It is important that teachers have proper education. To be sure, occasionally there arise some teachers who, though unschooled and untrained, nevertheless have an uncanny intuitive insight into Scripture. But such people are extremely rare. More often we face the problem of people calling themselves to the role of teacher who are simply not qualified to teach. A good teacher must have sound knowledge and the necessary skills to unravel difficult portions of Scripture. Here the need for mastery of language, history and theology are of critical importance.

If we examine the history of the Jewish people in the Old Testament, we see that one of the most severe and abiding threats to Israel was the threat of the false prophet or false teacher. More often than by the hand of the Philistines or the Assyrians, Israel fell to the seductive power of the lying teacher.

The New Testament bears witness to the same problem in the primitive Christian Church. The false prophet was like the hireling shepherd who was concerned more for his own wages than the welfare of the sheep. He thought nothing of misleading the people; leading them into error or to evil. Not all false prophets speak falsely out of malice; many do so out of ignorance. From the malicious and the ignorant we should flee.

On the other hand, one of the great blessings for Israel came when God sent them prophets and teachers who taught after his own mind. Hear the solemn warning God speaks to Jeremiah:

"I have heard what the prophets have said who prophesy falsely in My name, saying, 'I had a dream, I had a dream!' How long? Is there anything in the hearts of the prophets who prophesy falsehood, even these prophets of the deception of their own heart, who intend to make My people forget My name by their dreams which they relate to one another, just as their fathers forgot My name because of Baal? The prophet who has a dream may relate his dream, but let him who has My word speak My word in truth. What does straw have in common with grain?" declares the

LORD. *"Is not My word like fire?"* declares the LORD, *"and like a hammer which shatters a rock? Therefore behold, I am against the prophets,"* declares the LORD, *"who steal My words from each other. Behold, I am against the prophets,"* declares the LORD, *"who use their tongues and declare, 'The Lord declares.' Behold, I am against those who have prophesied false dreams,"* declares the LORD, *"and related them, and led My people astray by their falsehoods and reckless boasting; yet I did not send them or command them, nor do they furnish this people the slightest benefit,"* declares the LORD. (Jer. 23:25-32)

With words of judgment like these, it is not surprising that the New Testament warns, "Let not many *of you* become teachers, my brethren, knowing that as such we shall incur a stricter judgment" (Jas. 3:1). We need teachers who have sound knowledge and whose hearts are not set against the Word of God.

Private Bible study is an important means of grace for the Christian. It is a privilege and a duty for all of us. In his grace and kindness toward us God has provided not only gifted teachers in his church to assist us, but his own Holy Spirit to illumine his Word and search out its application to our lives. To sound teaching and diligent study God gives blessing.

3

Hermeneutics: The Science of Interpretation

Many of the modern controversies concerning the Bible re-
volve around questions concerning hermeneutics. The
science of hermeneutics is the science of biblical interpretation. In Greek mythology the god Hermes was the messenger
of the gods. It was his task to interpret the will of the gods.
Hence hermeneutics deals with conveying a message that
can be understood.

The purpose of hermeneutics is to establish guidelines
and rules for interpretation. It is a well developed science
that can become technical and complex. Any written document is subject to misinterpretation and thus we have
developed rules to safeguard us from such misunderstanding. We will restrict our present study to the most important
and basic rules and guidelines.

Historically the United States of America has a special
agency that theoretically functions as the supreme board of
hermeneutics for our land. That agency is called the
Supreme Court. One of its primary tasks is to interpret the

Constitution of the United States. The Constitution is a
written document and requires such interpretation. Originally the procedure of interpreting the Constitution followed the so-called grammatico-historical method. That is,
the Constitution was interpreted by studying the words of
the document itself in light of what those words meant when
they were used at the time of the formulation of the document.

Since the work of Oliver Wendell Holmes the method of
Constitutional interpretation has changed radically. The
current crisis in law and public confidence in the nation's
highest court is directly related to the underlying problem
of method of interpretation. When the court interprets the
Constitution in light of modern attitudes, it in effect changes
the Constitution by means of reinterpretation. The net result is that in a subtle way the Court becomes a legislative
rather than interpretive agency.

The same kind of crisis has occurred with biblical interpretation. When biblical scholars utilize the method of interpretation that involves "bringing the Bible up to date" by
reinterpretation, the original meaning of Scripture is obscured and the message is brought into conformity with contemporary trends in opinion.

The Analogy of Faith

When the Reformers broke with Rome and claimed the view
that the Bible was to be the supreme authority of the church
(*Sola Scriptura*), they were very careful to define basic
principles of interpretation. The primary rule of hermeneutics was called "the analogy of faith." The analogy of faith is
the rule that Scripture is to interpret Scripture: *Sacra Scriptura sui interpres* (Sacred Scripture is its own interpreter).
This means, quite simply, that no part of Scripture can be
interpreted in such a way as to render it in conflict with what
is clearly taught elsewhere in Scripture. For example, if a
given verse is capable of two renditions or variant interpretations and one of those interpretations goes against the
rest of Scripture while the other is in harmony with it,

then the latter interpretation must be used.

This principle rests on the prior confidence in the Bible as the inspired Word of God. It is, therefore, consistent and coherent. Since it is assumed that God would never contradict himself, it is thought slanderous to the Holy Spirit to choose an alternate interpretation that would unnecessarily bring the Bible in conflict with itself. In our own day such scrupulosity has been much abandoned by those who deny the inspiration of Scripture. It is commonplace to find modern interpreters who not only interpret Scripture against Scripture but go out of the way to do it. Efforts by orthodox scholars to harmonize difficult passages are ridiculed and largely ignored.

Quite apart from a question of inspiration, the analogy of faith method is a sound approach to interpret literature. The simple canons of common decency should protect any author from unwarranted charges of self-contradiction. If I have the option of interpreting a person's comments one of two ways, one rendering them consistent and the other contradictory, it seems that the person should get the benefit of the doubt.

I have had people ask me about passages I have written in books and say how can you say this in chapter 6 when in chapter 4 you say such and such. I then explain what I mean in chapter 6 and the person sees that the two thoughts are not ultimately in conflict. The perspective in chapter 6 is slightly different than in chapter 4, and at first glance the two seem in conflict, but by using the "philosophy of the second glance" the problem is resolved. We have all suffered from such misunderstanding and ought to be as sensitive to other people's words as we want them to be to our own.

It is, of course, conceivable that my words are contradictory: so this approach of sensitivity and the "benefit of the doubt philosophy" can be applied only when there is doubt. When there is no doubt that I have contradicted myself, there can only be critique. Nonetheless, when we do not try to interpret words in a consistent way, the words we read become a mass of confusion. When this happens in biblical interpretation, the Bible becomes a chameleon changing the color of its skin against the changing background of the people doing the interpreting.

Thus it is apparent that our view of the nature and origin of the Bible will have a significant effect on how we go about interpreting it. If the Bible is the inspired Word of God, then the analogy of faith is not an option but a requirement of interpretation.

Interpreting the Bible Literally

"You don't take the Bible literally, do you?" is a question I am often asked. The way it is phrased and the tone of voice with which it is expressed betrays that it is not a question but an accusation. The implied meaning is, "You certainly aren't so naive as to interpret the Bible literally in this day and age, are you?" When I hear this question, I feel like I am being unceremoniously deposited in the archives of the Scopes monkey trial.

When I get such questions I respond to them with a standard reply. I do not say, "Yes," or even, "Well, sometimes." Rather I answer, "Of course." (Meaning: who in their right mind would not interpret the Bible literally?) I do this as a sort of shock to draw people's attention to the real meaning of literal interpretation of the Bible.

One of the most significant advances of biblical scholarship during the Reformation was gained as a result of Luther's militant advocacy of the second rule of hermeneutics: The Bible should be interpreted according to its literal sense. This was Luther's principle of interpreting the Bible by its *sensus literalis*. To understand what was meant by this emphasis on the literal sense we need to examine the historical situation in which it arose and the meaning of the words themselves. (Now I have to be involved in a grammatico-historical interpretation of Luther!)

The term *literal* comes from the Latin *litera* meaning letter. To interpret something literally is to pay attention to the *litera* or to the letters and words which are being used. To interpret the Bible literally is to interpret it as *literature*. That is, the natural meaning of a passage is to be interpreted according to the normal rules of grammar, speech, syntax and context.

The Bible may be a very special book, being uniquely inspired by the Holy Ghost, but that inspiration does not transform the letters of the words or the sentences of the passages into magical phrases. Under inspiration a noun remains a noun and a verb remains a verb. Questions do not become exclamations, and historical narratives do not become allegories. Luther's principle was anything but magical or simplistic. The principle of literal interpretation is a principle that calls for the closest kind of literary scrutiny of the text. To be accurate interpreters of the Bible we need to know the rules of grammar; and above all, we must be carefully involved in what is called *genre analysis*.

Literal Interpretation and Genre Analysis

The term *genre* means simply "kind," "sort" or "species." Genre analysis involves the study of such things as literary forms, figures of speech and style. We do this with all kinds of literature. We distinguish between lyric poetry and legal briefs, between newspaper accounts of current events and epic poems. We distinguish between the style of historical narratives and sermons, between realistic graphic description and hyperbole. Failure to make these distinctions when dealing with the Bible can lead to a host of problems with interpretation. Literary analysis is crucial to accurate interpretation. A few examples of how this works out in biblical matters may be helpful.

The problem of historicity of Jonah often centers around questions of literary analysis. Many scholars who believe in the infallibility of the Bible do not believe that Jonah was actually swallowed by a whale (or a great fish).

Because a lengthy section of the book of Jonah is written in a style that is clearly poetic (the entire second chapter), some maintain that the book never had any intention of conveying the idea that the incident actually happened in history. Rather Jonah is seen as a kind of epic or dramatic poem that is not designed to communicate history. Thus, since the

book does not purport to be historical, we ought not to take it
as history. Other scholars reject the historicity of Jonah on
other grounds. They argue that the book does purport to be
a historical narrative with the poetic section merely reflect-
ing Jonah's prayer of thanksgiving for rescue from the
sea but should not be taken seriously because it involves a
miracle of nature. Since these scholars do not believe
miracles can happen, they reject the historicity of the book.
Thus, the first group rejects the historicity of Jonah on
literary grounds while the second does it on philosophical-
theological grounds.

Literary analysis cannot decide philosophical questions of
whether or not Jonah could have been swallowed by a fish.
All it can do is give us some basis to decide whether someone
was actually claiming that such an event took place. If a person does not believe that miracles are possible, he has no
grounds to argue that someone else could not *say* that one
took place (unless, of course, it took a miracle to claim a
miracle took place!).

Another example of problems arising out of literary conflicts may be seen in the biblical use of hyperbole. *Hyperbole*
means etymologically "an overshooting." One dictionary
defines it as "a statement exaggerated fancifully, as for
effect." The use of hyperbole is a common linguistic phenomenon. For example, the New Testament writers say, "And
Jesus was going about all the cities and the villages, teaching . . ." (Mt. 9:35). Does the author mean to convey that
every single village was visited? Perhaps, but it is doubtful.

We use language in the same way. When the Pittsburgh
Steelers won the Super Bowl for the first time, the fans
turned out in multitudes to celebrate the victory and welcome the team home. Some newsmen said, "The whole city
turned out to greet them." Did the newsman expect people to
understand that every single resident of Pittsburgh was
there? Of course not. His words were obviously meant to be
hyperbolic.

I know of one very competent Bible scholar who rejects
the notion of the inerrancy of the Bible because Jesus made a

mistake when he said the mustard seed was the smallest of seeds. Since we know that there are seeds smaller than the mustard seed, we see that Jesus and the New Testament erred by saying it was the smallest. But to accuse Jesus or the Scripture of error when hyperbole is clearly in use is to fail to be involved in literary analysis.

Literary analysis can also untangle some confusion that results from personification. Personification is a poetic device by which inanimate objects or animals are given human characteristics. The impersonal is described in personal terms. The Bible describes the hills as dancing and clapping their hands. Such figures of speech are usually easy to recognize and cause no difficulty in interpretation. In some cases, however, questions of personification have led to serious debate. For example, the Old Testament records the incident of Balaam's ass speaking. Is this a sudden intrusion of a poetic form in the midst of a historical narrative? Does the speaking animal indicate the presence of fable in the text? Or do we find here an indication of a miracle or special providence recorded as part of the record of divine activity in history?

The subjective way to answer these questions is to prejudge them from a viewpoint that allows or disallows miracles. An objective way to answer the question of what is being said is to apply literary standards to the text. This particular episode takes place in the midst of a section of Scripture that does not bear the marks of poetry or fable. The immediate context bears all the marks of historical narrative. The ass speaking, however, is a significant aspect of the total text, so it presents some problems. Again, the purpose of this discussion is not to decide whether the ass spoke or not but to illustrate how the matter of personification may lead to controversy.

If we call something personification that has all the marks of historical narrative, we are guilty of eisogesis. If the Bible claims something actually happened, we have no right to "explain it away" by calling it personification. That is a literary and intellectual cop-out. If we don't believe it happened, let us say so and view it as an intrusion of primitive superstition in the Old Testament record.

A question of personification that has engendered rabid controversy is the speaking serpent in the Genesis account of the Fall. The Dutch Reformed Church in the Netherlands has gone through a serious crisis revolving around a leading theological professor's view of this. When Karl Barth visited the Netherlands during the height of this controversy, he was asked, "Did the snake speak?" Barth replied, "What did the snake say?" Barth's clever response was designed to say, "It doesn't matter whether the snake spoke. What matters is what it said and what the impact of the words were in this description of the Fall. Of course Barth was right if the biblical account of the Fall is neither historical nor purports to be historical. His answer, however, did not satisfy the Dutch people because their concern was not so much over whether or not there was a snake who really spoke but over the reasons why their professor denied the historicity of the account.

The opening chapters of Genesis provide real difficulty to the person who wants to pinpoint the precise literary genre used. Part of the text has the earmarks of historical literature, yet part of it exhibits the kind of imagery found in symbolic literature. Adam is placed in a real geographical location and is portrayed as a real human being. Most significantly, he is placed in the framework of a family genealogy which to the Jew would be most inappropriate for a mythical character. Adam is grouped elsewhere in Scripture alongside other personages whose historical reality is in no wise in doubt. All of this would be weighty reason under the canons of literary analysis to view Adam as a historical character. (There are, of course, additional theological reasons to do so, but we are concerned here only with the question of literary analysis.) However, in addition to the presence of clear historical narrative characteristics, we find references, for example, to the Tree of the Knowledge of Good and Evil in the Garden. What kind of a tree is that? What kind of leaves did it have; what kind of fruit did it bear? This image has the characteristics of a kind of symbolism found, for example, in apocalyptic literature such as the book of Revelation.

Thus, in the opening chapters of the Bible we are confronted with a kind or form of literature which has elements of historical narrative and elements of symbolism mixed in an unusual way. Only after we determine what kind of literature it is can we discern what it is communicating to us as history. After that is decided, then we can move to the question of its credibility. At the risk of being repetitious, let me emphasize once more that we must be careful to note the difference between discerning what the Bible is actually saying and the question of whether what it it saying is true or not.

The Problem of Metaphor

A metaphor is a figure of speech in which a word or a phrase literally denoting one kind of object or idea is used in place of another to suggest a likeness or analogy between them. The Bible frequently makes use of metaphors, and they are found often on the lips of Jesus. Again, in most cases they are relatively easy to discern. When Jesus says, "I am the door; if anyone enters through Me, he shall be saved" (Jn. 10:9), how are we to understand that? Does that mean that where we have skin Jesus has mahogany veneer? Where we have arms Jesus has hinges? Where we have a navel Jesus has a doorknob? Such conclusions are, of course, absurd. Here Jesus uses the form of the verb *to be* in a metaphorical way.

But what does he mean when he says at the Last Supper, "This is My body" (Lk. 22:19)? Did the bread represent his body in a metaphorical way? Or did it become his body in a real and "literal" way? In this case the literary form is not so obvious. Differences in literary analysis have led to serious divisions in the church over the meaning of the Lord's Supper. One of the very few issues over which Luther and Calvin were never able to reach agreement was the very matter of the meaning of these words of Jesus. At one point in negotiations between representatives of Calvin and

Luther, Luther kept repeating, "*Hoc est corpus meum; hoc est corpus meum. . . .*" (This is my body. . . .) Surely, given both Luther and Calvin's view of the authority of the Bible, if they could have agreed as to what the Bible was actually saying, they both would have submitted to it.

Thus, the classical method of seeking the literal sense of Scripture meant seeking a knowledge of what is being communicated through the various forms and figures of speech employed in biblical literature. This was done not with a view to soften or weaken or relativize the Scriptures but to understand them correctly that they might serve more effectively as a guide to the faith and practice of God's people.

The Medieval Quadriga

Though Luther was not the first to stress the importance of seeking the literal sense of Scripture, he made the biggest dent in the prevailing method of interpretation of his day which followed the so-called *quadriga*. The quadriga was the fourfold method of interpretation that had its roots very early in church history. From the work of Clement and Origen onward it is commonplace to find biblical commentators using a fanciful method of allegorizing in their biblical interpretation. By the Middle Ages the fourfold method was firmly established. This method examined each text for four meanings: literal, moral, allegorical and anagogical.

The literal sense of Scripture was defined as the plain and evident meaning. The moral sense was that which instructed men how to behave. The allegorical sense revealed the content of faith, and the anagogical expressed future hope. Thus passages, for example, which mentioned Jerusalem were capable of four different meanings. The literal sense referred to the capital of Judea and the central sanctuary of the nation. The moral sense of Jerusalem is the soul of man (the "central sanctuary" of man). The allegorical meaning of Jerusalem is the church (the center of the Christian community). The anagogical meaning is heaven (the final hope of future residence for the people of God). Thus, a single reference to Jerusalem could mean four different things at the same time. If the Bible mentioned that someone went up to Jerusalem, it meant that they went to a real earthly city, or that their souls "went up" to a place of moral excellence, or that we should go to church or that we will someday go up to heaven.

It is amazing how far intelligent people went with such a bizarre method of interpretation. Even Augustine and Aquinas, who favored restricting theology to the literal sense, nevertheless often speculated wildly via the *quadriga*. One need only glance at Augustine's allegorical treatment of the parable of the good Samaritan to see this method in operation. By peering beneath the surface of the plain sense of Scriptures, biblical exegetes came up with all sorts of odd things. Against this as well as other abuses, Martin Luther protested.

Though Luther rejected multiple meanings to biblical passages, he did not thereby restrict the application of Scripture to a single sense. Though a scriptural passage has one meaning, it may have a host of applications to the wide variety of nuances to our lives. I know one seminary professor who gave his students an assignment on the first day of class to read one verse of the New Testament and write down fifty things they learned from the study of that verse. The students worked long into the night, feverishly comparing notes in order to meet the requirements of the professor. When they returned to class the next morning the professor acknowledged their labor and assigned them fifty more from the same passage for the following day. The point, of course, was to burn into the students' minds the wealth and depth of truth to be found in a single passage of Scripture. The professor was dramatizing that, though Scripture has a unified meaning, its *application* can be rich and varied.

Both the analogy of faith and the principle of seeking the literal sense (*sensus literalis*) are necessary safeguards against unbridled speculation and subjectivistic interpretation. As defined, the literal sense is not meant to indicate a crass, rigid forcing of the whole Bible into a pattern of historical narrative. It is a safeguard, in fact, against doing that very thing as well as against redefining the Bible by imposing figurative meanings on passages not meant to be figurative. We can distort the Bible in either direction. One method may be more sophisticated than the other, but no less distortive.

The Grammatico-Historical Method

Closely related to the analogy of faith and the literal sense of Scripture is the method of interpretation called the grammatico-historical method. As the name suggests, this method focuses attention not only on literary forms but upon grammatical constructions and historical contexts out of which the Scriptures were written. Written statements come to us within a grammatical structure of some sort. Poetry has certain rules of structure, as do business letters. When dealing with Scripture, it is important to know the difference between a direct object and a predicate nominative or predicate adjective. Not only is it important to know English grammar but helpful to know some of the peculiarities of Hebrew and Greek grammar. If, for example, the American public had a thorough knowledge of Greek grammar, the Jehovah Witnesses would have a much more difficult time selling their interpretation of the first chapter of the Gospel of John by which the Witnesses deny the deity of Christ.

Grammatical structure determines whether words are to be taken as questions (interrogative), commands (imperative) or declarative (indicative). For example, when Jesus says, "You shall be My witnesses" (Acts 1:8), is he making a prediction of future performance, or is he issuing a sovereign mandate? The English form is unclear. The Greek structure of the words, however, makes it perfectly clear that Jesus is not indulging in future prediction but is issuing a command.

Other ambiguities of language can be cleared up and elucidated by acquiring a working knowledge of grammar. For example, when Paul says at the beginning of his Epistle to the Romans that he is an apostle called to communicate "the gospel of God," what does he mean by *of*? Does the *of* refer to the content of that gospel or its source? Does *of* really mean "about," or is it a genitive of possession? The grammatical answer will determine whether Paul is saying that he is going to communicate the gospel *about* God or whether he is saying he is going to communicate a gospel that comes *from* God and belongs to God. There is a big difference between the two that can only be resolved by grammatical analysis. In this case the Greek structure reveals a genitive of possession which answers the question for us.

Historical analysis involves seeking a knowledge of the setting and situation in which the books of the Bible were written. This is a requisite for understanding what the Bible meant in its historical context. This matter of historical investigation is as dangerous as it is necessary. The dangers of it will be spelled out later in chapter 5. The necessity is there for a proper understanding of what has been said. Questions of authorship, date and destination of books are important for a clear understanding of a book. If we know who wrote a book, to whom, under what circumstances, at what period in history, that information will greatly ease our difficulty in understanding it.

For example, there are many very difficult and problematic passages in the Epistle to the Hebrews. The difficulties are compounded because we do not know for sure who wrote the book, who the "Hebrews" addressed were and, most importantly, what particular form of apostasy threatened the lives of the community addressed. If one or more of those questions could be answered with certainty, we could go a long way in unraveling the special problems the book presents.

Source Criticism

The method of so-called source criticism has been helpful in some respects in shedding light on the Scriptures. Following the notion that Mark was the first Gospel written and that Matthew and Luke had Mark's Gospel in front of them as they wrote, many of the questions of the relationship of the Gospels can be explained. We see further that both Luke and Matthew include certain information that is not found in Mark. Thus, it seems that Luke and Matthew had a source of information available to them that Mark did not have or did not choose to use. Examining further, we find certain information found in Matthew that is found in neither Mark nor Luke, and information that is in Luke that is found only in Luke. By isolating the material found only in Matthew or only in Luke, we can discern certain things about their priorities and concerns in writing. Knowing why an author writes what he writes helps us to understand what he writes. In contemporary reading it is important to read the author's preface because the reasons and concerns for writing are usually spelled out there.

By using methods of source criticism we can isolate materials common to particular writers. For example, almost all the information we have in the New Testament about Joseph, the husband of Mary, is found in Matthew's Gospel. Why? Or why does Matthew have so many more references to the Old Testament than the other Gospels? The answer is obvious. Matthew is writing to a Jewish audience. It was the Jews who had legal questions of Jesus' claim to Messiahship. Jesus' legal father was Joseph, and that was very important for Matthew to show in order to establish the tribal lineage of Jesus.

By the same kind of analysis we discover that Luke is obviously writing his Gospel for a wider audience than Matthew and is very much concerned with communicating to the gentile world. He stresses, for example, the "universality" of the application of the gospel.

Authorship and Dating

Questions of authorship and date are also important to a proper understanding of the text. Since language can change its meaning from one generation to another and from differing localities, it is important to be as precise as possible in fixing the place and date of a book. Such efforts to date and assign authorship have been a major factor in theological controversy because of some of the methods employed.

When questions of dating are approached strictly from a naturalistic perspective, books that claim to include predictive prophecy are placed at a date contemporary with or after the events they have predicted. Here we see extraliterary and historical criteria being improperly imposed on the books.

Matters of authorship and dating are closely linked. If we know who wrote a particular book and know when that person lived, then, of course, we know the basic period when the book was written. This is why scholars argue so much about who wrote Isaiah or 2 Timothy. If Isaiah wrote Isaiah, then we are dealing with an amazing piece of predictive prophecy that would require a high view of inspiration. If Isaiah did not write the whole book that bears his name, then a lower view of Scripture could be justified.

It has been almost amusing to see the way Paul's letters have been treated by higher critics of the modern era. Poor Paul has had almost every one of his Epistles alternately taken away from him and then given back. One of the least scientific methods used to criticize authorship is the study of what is called the incidence of *hapax legomena*. The phrase *hapax legomena* refers to the appearance of words in a particular book that are found nowhere else in the author's writings. For example, if we find 36 words in Ephesians that are found nowhere else in any of Paul's writings, we might conclude that Paul did not or could not have written Ephesians.

The folly of putting too much stock in *hapax legomena* came home to me when I had to learn the Dutch language in a hurry for my graduate work in the Netherlands. I studied Dutch by the "inductive method." I was assigned several volumes of theology written by G. C. Berkouwer. I started my study by reading his volume on *The Person of Christ* which was in Dutch. I started on the first page with the first word and looked it up in the dictionary. I wrote the Dutch word on one side of a card and the English word on the other side and set about the task of learning Berkouwer's vocabulary. After doing this on every page of *The Person of Christ,* I had over 6,000 words on cards. The next volume I studied was Berkouwer's *The Work of Christ*. I found over 3,000 words in that book that were not found in the first one. That's significant evidence that *The Work of Christ* was not written by Berkouwer! Note that Berkouwer wrote *The Work of Christ* only one year after he wrote *The Person of Christ*. He was dealing with the same general theme (Christology) and writing to the same general audience, yet there were thousands of words found in the second volume that were not found in the first.

Note also that the quantity of Berkouwer's writing in the first volume far exceeds the total quantity of writing that survives from the pen of the Apostle Paul. Paul's letters were much more brief. They were written to a wide variety of audiences, covering a wide diversity of subjects and issues, and were written over a long period of time. Yet people get excited when they find a handful of words in a given Epistle that are found nowhere else. Unless Paul had the vocabulary of a six-year-old and had no literary talent whatsoever, we should pay little attention to such unbridled speculation.

To recap, sound interpretation demands a careful analysis of the grammar and historical context of a writing. This work must be done. Higher critics have done much to advance our knowledge of linguistic, grammatical and historical background for the Bible. Sometimes the naturalistic assumptions many of them use cast a shadow over much of their work. But the analysis is necessary. And only through this kind of analysis can we have the necessary checks to restrain those scholars who do get carried away.

Grammatical Errors
Before we move on to basic practical principles of interpretation, let me mention one more problem concerning grammar. A close analysis of grammatical structures used in the New Testament has raised more than a few eyebrows concerning the Bible's inspiration. When we look at the book of Revelation, we find a style of writing that is coarse and crude in its grammatical structure. We see numerous "errors" of grammar manifested. This has provoked some to attack the

notion of inspiration as well as the notion of the inerrancy of Scripture. But both principles of inspiration and inerrancy allow for grammatical error as the principles have been formulated. The Bible is not written in "Holy Ghost Greek." Inspiration never meant for Protestant orthodoxy that the Spirit "dictated" the words and the "style" of the human authors. Nor were the authors viewed as machine-like automatons totally passive to the Spirit's operation. Nor did inerrancy mean to preclude grammatical errors. Inerrancy is used to indicate the "utter truthfulness" of the Scripture. When Luther says the Scriptures never err, he means that they never err with respect to the truth of what they are proclaiming. We can see this in the jury system of our own country with reference to the crime of perjury. If an innocent man is asked about his guilt on the witness stand and he replies, "I ain't killed nobody notime," he cannot be charged with perjury because he used bad grammar to state his case.

The three primary principles of interpretation are aids to our personal enrichment. The analogy of faith keeps the whole Bible in view lest we suffer from the effects of exaggerating one part of Scripture to the exclusion of others. The literal sense offers a restraint from letting our imaginations run away in fanciful interpretation and invites us to examine closely the literary forms of Scripture. The grammatico-historical method focuses our attention on the original meaning of the text lest we "read into Scripture" our own ideas drawn from the present. We turn now to a consideration of how these principles apply in actual practice.

4

Practical Rules for Biblical Interpretation

In this chapter we will attempt to set forth the most basic and necessary practical rules for interpreting the Bible. These rules rest upon the principles set forth in the preceding chapter.

Rule 1: The Bible Is to Be Read Like Any Other Book
This rule goes at the beginning because it is so important. It is also a rule that is easy to misunderstand. When I say we must read the Bible as we would any other book, I do not mean that the Bible is like other books in every respect. I believe the Bible is uniquely inspired and infallible, and this puts it in a class by itself. But for matters of interpretation the Bible does not take on some special magic that changes basic literary patterns of interpretation. This rule is simply the application of the principle of *sensus literalis*. In the Bible a verb is a verb and a noun is a noun, just as in any other book.

But if the Bible is to be interpreted like any other book,

what about prayer? Shouldn't we seek the assistance of God the Holy Spirit in interpreting the Book? Isn't divine illumination promised to this book in a way that differs from other books?

When we raise questions about prayer and divine illumination, we enter into areas in which the Bible is indeed different from other books. For the spiritual benefit of applying the words of Scripture to our lives, prayer is enormously helpful. To illumine the spiritual significance of a text the Holy Ghost is quite important. But to discern the difference between historical narrative and metaphor, prayer is not a great help unless it involves earnest supplication to God to give us clear minds and pure hearts to overcome our prejudices. Sanctification of the heart is vital for our minds to be free to hear what the Word is saying. We should also pray that God will assist us to overcome our proclivity for slothfulness and make us diligent students of Scripture. But mystical flashes are usually not very helpful in the basic work of exegesis. Even worse is the so-called spiritual method of "luckydipping."

"Luckydipping" refers to the method of Bible study in which a person prays for divine guidance and then lets the Bible fall open to wherever it happens to open. Then, with eyes shut the person "dips" his finger to the page and gets his answer from God wherever the finger lands on the page. I remember one Christian girl who came to me in a state of ecstasy in her senior year of college. She was experiencing the throes of "senior panic" as she was nearing graduation with no prospect of marriage in sight. She had been praying diligently for a husband and finally resorted to luckydipping for an answer from God. With this method her finger came to rest on Zechariah 9:9:

Rejoice greatly, O daughter of Zion!
Shout in triumph, *O daughter of Jerusalem!*
Behold, your king is coming to you;
He is just and endowed with salvation,
Humble, and mounted on a donkey,
Even on a colt, the foal of a donkey.

With this direct word from God, the girl was sure that she was headed for the marriage altar and that her prince was on the way. Maybe he wasn't coming on a big white horse, but a donkey was close enough.

This is not a sound way to use the Bible. I don't think that either Zechariah or the Holy Ghost had this in mind when the words were penned. I am embarrassed to say, however, that about a week later our young lady started dating a fellow that she married within a few months! I think that had more to do with her new confidence in dating that she got through a bad means than through the providence of God confirming a divine promise.

Rule 2: Read the Bible Existentially

I mention this rule in a spirit of fear and trembling. This rule could be grossly distorted and become more trouble than help. Before I define what I do mean by it, let me define clearly what I do not mean.

I do not mean that we should use the modern "existential" method of interpreting Scripture whereby the words of Scripture are taken out of their historical context for subjective meaning. Rudolf Bultmann, for example, advocates a kind of existential hermeneutic by which he seeks what he calls "punctiliar" revelation. Here revelation takes place not on the plane of history but rather in the moment of my own personal decision. God speaks to me in the "*hic et nunc*" (the here and now). In this approach, what actually took place in history is not of prime importance. What matters is a "theology of timelessness." We often hear scholars of this school saying to us that it doesn't really matter whether Jesus even lived in history. What matters is the message to us now. Jesus can "mean" not a person in history but a symbol of "liberation."

The problem with this approach is that it really does matter whether or not Jesus really lived, died and was resurrected in history. As Paul argues in 1 Corinthians 15, if Christ be not raised, "our faith is worthless." Without a real historical resurrection, we are left with a dead savior and a powerless gospel. The good news would end with death, not life. Thus, by this rule, I am in no way endorsing the modern relativistic, subjectivistic and anti-historical method of interpretation of the existentialists. I am using the term existential in a different way.

What I mean is that as we read the Bible, we ought to get passionately and personally involved in what we read. I advocate this not only for the purpose of personal application of the text but for understanding as well. What I am calling for is a kind of empathy by which we try to "crawl into the skin" of the characters we are reading about.

Much of biblical history comes to us by way of understatement and remarkable brevity. Consider the following narrative:

> *Now Nadab and Abihu, the sons of Aaron, took their respective firepans, and after putting fire in them, placed incense on it and offered strange fire before the LORD, which He had not commanded them. And fire came out from the presence of the LORD and consumed them, and they died before the LORD. Then Moses said to Aaron, "It is what the Lord spoke, saying, 'By those who come near Me I will be treated as holy, and before all the people I will be honored.'" So Aaron, therefore, kept silent. (Lev. 10:1-3)*

What is going on here? In three short verses the drama of sin and subsequent execution of Aaron's sons are briefly recorded. Little is said of Aaron's reaction. All we read is that Moses interpreted the reasons for God's judgment and that Aaron, therefore, kept silent. What was Aaron thinking when he saw his sons wiped out? Can we read between the lines a bit? If he were like me, he was thinking, "What is going on? C'mon, God, I've been working for you all this time, sacrificing my life to you and you wiped out my sons for a childish prank. It isn't fair." That would be my reaction. But if I so reacted and the Holy God of Israel sharply reminded me of the sanctity of the altar and the seriousness of the priestly task, by saying, "By those who come near Me I will be treated as holy, and before all the people I will be honored," I would shut my mouth in a hurry, too.

By trying to put ourselves in the life situation of the characters of Scripture, we can come to a better understanding of what we are reading. This is the practice of empathy, feeling the emotions of the characters we are studying. Such reading between the lines may not be regarded as part of the text of Scripture itself but will aid in our understanding the flavor of what is happening.

In *Fear and Trembling* Sören Kierkegaard speculates on the narrative of Abraham's sacrifice of Isaac. He asks himself, "Why did Abraham get up early in the morning to sacrifice his son?" He considers the text from a series of possible answers to that question. When he is finished, the reader feels as if he has been to Mount Moriah and back with Abraham. Here the drama of the narrative is captured. Again, such speculation adds nothing to the authoritative interpretation of what the text actually says, but it gives us a handle on our understanding of it. This is why "reading between the lines" is a legitimate enterprise in preaching.

Kierkegaard's dramatic treatment of Abraham was stimulated by the question, Why did Abraham do what he did? In reading Scripture we are often confounded and even outraged by what we read, particularly when we read of some example of severe judgment imposed by God. It would appear from time to time that God visits cruel and unusual punishment on his people. Many such problems can be cleared up if we just stop and ask calmly, "Why does God do this?" or "Why does Scripture say this?" When we do this, we help ourselves over the prejudice we have by nature against God.

When I am annoyed at someone, it is often difficult for me to hear what he is saying or to understand what he is doing. When I am angry, I tend to interpret the person who is the object of my wrath in the worst possible light. Note how often we do that with Scripture. Every time I lecture on divine election, invariably someone will say, "Do you mean that God arbitrarily treats us like puppets?" I am offended that anyone would jump to the conclusion that I had such a notion of God. I had not said it, nor did my words intend to imply it, yet the notion of any kind of divine sovereignty seems so repugnant that people put it in the worst possible light.

We are faced with a commonplace human tendency and we are all guilty of it: we tend to view the actions and words of those we dislike in the worst possible light and to view our own shortcomings in the best possible light. When a person sins against me, I respond as if he were purely malicious; when I sin against him, I "make a mistake of judgment." If we are by nature at enmity with God, we have to guard against this inclination when we approach his Word.

In light of the current controversy concerning the role of women in the church, the Apostle Paul has really taken a beating. I have read literature describing Paul as a male chauvinist, a misogynist and an anti-feminist. Some people have so much hostility for Paul on this matter that venom drips from their pens and they can't hear a word he says. By using this existential method of empathy, we may gain a better understanding of Paul the man but more importantly of what he actually says.

Adela Rogers St. John writes of a fictional character who wanted to read the New Testament Epistles for the first time. In order to get a "virgin" reaction to them he had his secretary sit down and type up each Epistle, address the Epistle to him, and send them in the mail to his house. He would then read each Epistle as if it had been written to him. That's the empathetic method.

Rule 3: Historical Narratives Are to Be Interpreted by the Didactic

We have already examined the basic characteristics of historical narrative forms. Before we can understand this rule, we must give definition to the didactic form. The term *didactic* comes from the Greek word that means to teach or to instruct. Didactic literature is literature that teaches or explains. Much of Paul's writing is didactic in character. The relationship between the Gospels and the Epistles often has been defined in the simple terms of saying that the Gospels record what Jesus did and the Epistles interpret the significance of what he did. Such a description is an oversimplification in that the Gospels often teach and interpret as they are giving narration. But it is true that the emphasis in the Gospels is found in the record of events, while the Epistles are more concerned with interpreting the significance of those events in terms of doctrine, exhortation and application.

Since the Epistles are largely interpretative and come after the Gospels in order of organization, the Reformers maintained the principle that the Epistles should interpret the Gospels rather than the Gospels interpret the Epistles. This rule is not absolute but is a helpful rule of thumb. This order of interpretation is puzzling to many since the Gospels record not only the acts of Jesus but his teaching as well. Does not this mean that Jesus' words and teaching are given less authority than the apostles? That is certainly not the intent of the principle. Neither the Epistles nor the Gospels were given superior authority over the other by the Reformers. Rather the Gospels and Epistles have equal authority, though there may be a difference in the order of interpretation.

Since the erosion of confidence in biblical authority in our day, it has been fashionable to put the authority of Jesus over against the authority of the Epistles, particularly of Paul's Epistles. People do not seem to realize that they are not setting Jesus against Paul so much as they are setting one apostle such as Matthew or John over against another. We must remember that Jesus wrote none of the New Testament, and we are dependent upon apostolic testimony for our knowledge of what he did and said.

Not long ago I was reunited with a very close friend from my college days. We hadn't seen each other for almost twenty years, and we chatted to bring each other up to date. In the course of our conversation he told me how his mind had changed on many issues. He particularly mentioned how his views on the nature and authority of Scripture had changed. He said he no longer believed that the Bible was inspired, and he took umbrage with some of the teachings found there, especially some of Paul's teaching.

I asked him what he still believed that hadn't changed.

He replied, "I still believe that Jesus is my Lord and Savior."

"How does Jesus exercise lordship over your life?" I asked him gently. He didn't quite understand what I was getting at until I refined the question a bit. I asked him how Jesus transmitted any information that would be part of the content of his rule. I said, "Jesus said, 'If you love me, keep my commandments.' I see that you still love him and want to be obedient to him, but where do you find his commandments? If Paul doesn't communicate the will of Christ accurately and the other apostles are equally errant, how do you discover the will of your Lord?"

He hesitated for a moment and then replied, "In the decisions of the church when it meets in council."

I didn't bother to ask which church or which council, since so many disagree. I merely pointed out that perhaps it was time we made another visit to the Diet of Worms. Many Protestants have forgotten what they are protesting and have come full circle to the point of elevating the present decisions of the church over the authority of the apostles. When that happens, we have an upside-down Christianity. If we can trust the Gospel writers at all, perhaps we can trust their accuracy when they record that Jesus called the prophets and the apostles the foundation of the church. In my friend's mind that foundation has been destroyed and a new one laid in its place: the contemporary opinions of churchmen.

If Paul and Peter and the other New Testament authors received their authority as apostles from Jesus himself, how can we criticize them in their teaching and still claim to follow Christ? This is the same issue that Jesus took up with the Pharisees. They claimed to honor God while they rejected the One God sent and bore witness to. They claimed to be children of Abraham while they rued the One who caused Abraham to rejoice. They appealed to the authority of Moses while rejecting the One of whom Moses wrote.

Irenaeus raised the same point against the gnostics of the early church who attacked the authority of the apostles. He said, if you don't obey the apostles, you can't be obedient to God, because, if you reject the apostles, you reject the One who sent them (Jesus); and, if you reject the One who sent the apostles, you reject the One who sent him (God the Father). Thus, against the gnostics, Irenaeus merely took Jesus' argument with the Pharisees one step further.

Thus the principle of interpreting the narrative by the didactic is not designed to set apostle against apostle or apostle against Christ. It is merely recognizing one of the principle tasks of the apostle, to teach and to interpret the mind of Christ for his people.

One of the chief reasons why this rule is important is to warn against drawing too many inferences from records of what people do. For example, can we really construct a manual of required Christian behavior purely on the basis of an analysis of what Jesus did? So often when a Christian is faced with a problematic situation, he is told to ask himself, "What would Jesus do in this situation?" That is not always a wise question to ask. A better question would be, "What would Jesus have me do in this situation?"

Why is it dangerous to simply try to model our lives after what Jesus did? If we try to model our lives precisely according to Jesus' example, we may get into trouble on several counts. First of all, our tasks as obedient children to God are not exactly the same as Jesus' mission. I was not sent into this world to save men from their sins. I can never speak with absolute authority about anything like Jesus did. I cannot go into the church with a whip and drive corrupt clergymen out. I am not the Lord of the church.

Second, and perhaps not so obviously, Jesus lived under a different period of redemptive history than I do. He was required to fulfill all the laws of the Old Covenant including dietary and ceremonial laws. Jesus was being perfectly obedient to the Father when he was circumcised as a religious rite. If I become circumcised, not for reasons of health or hygiene but as a formal religious rite, I am, by that rite, repudiating the finished work of Christ and bringing myself back under the curse of the Old Testament law. In other words, we could be guilty of serious sin if we tried to imitate Jesus exactly. Here is where the Epistles are so very important. They do call us to imitate Christ at many points. But they help us to delineate what those points are and what they are not.

A third problem with emulating the life of Jesus is in making the subtle move from what is permissible to what is obligatory. For example, I know men who argue that it is the Christian's duty to make visitations of mercy on the Sabbath day. The argument is that Jesus did it on the Sabbath day and therefore we should.

Now the subtlety is here: that Jesus did such things on the Sabbath reveals that such activities do not violate the Sabbath and are good. But Jesus nowhere commands us to do them on the Sabbath. His example shows that they may be done, but not necessarily that they must be done then. He does command us to visit the sick, but nowhere stipulates when that visitation must take place. That Jesus remained unmarried shows that celibacy is good, but his celibacy does not demand that marriage be repudiated, as the Epistles make clear.

There is another serious problem with drawing too many inferences from narratives. The Bible records not only the virtues of the saints but their vices as well. The portraits of the saints are painted wart and all. We have to be careful not to emulate the "wartiness." To be sure when we read of the activities of David or Paul, we can learn much since these are the activities of men who achieved a high degree of sanctification. But should we emulate the adultery of David or the dishonesty of Jacob? God forbid.

Apart from extrapolating points of character and ethics from the narratives, there is also the problem of extracting doctrine. For example, in the narrative of Abraham's offering Isaac on the altar at Mount Moriah, he is stopped at the last second by an angel from God who says, "Abraham, Abraham! Do not stretch out your hand against the lad, and do nothing to him; for now I know that you fear God, since you have not withheld your son, your only son, from Me" (Gen. 22:11-12). Note the words, "now I know." Didn't God know in advance what Abraham was going to do? Did he sit in heaven in a state of divine anxiety awaiting the outcome of Abraham's trial? Did he pace up and down the celestial quarters asking for bulletins from the angels on the progress of the drama? Of course not. The didactic portions of Scripture preclude such inferences. Yet, if we established our doctrine of God purely from narratives such as this one, we would have to conclude that our God is "ever learning and never coming to a knowledge of the truth."

Building doctrine from narratives alone is dangerous business. I am sad to say that there appears to be a strong tendency for this in the popular evangelical theology of our day. We all must be careful to resist this tendency.

The Problem of Phenomenological Language in Historical Narrative.   The Bible is written in human language. It is the only kind of language that we can understand because we are humans. The limitations of human language apply throughout the Bible. In fact, much has been written in recent years about this problem. Skepticism has sometimes reached the point of declaring that all human language is inadequate to express God's truth. Such skepticism is unwarranted at best and cynical at worst. Our language may not be perfect, but it is adequate.

Nonetheless, these limitations become apparent when we deal with phenomenological language, especially in historical narratives. Phenomenological language is that language which describes things as they appear to the naked eye. When biblical writers describe the universe around them, they do it in terms of external appearances and not with a view to scientific, technological precision.

How many controversies have boiled over whether or not the Bible teaches that the Earth rather than the sun is the center of the solar system? Remember Galileo who was excommunicated because he taught heliocentricity (sun-centered solar system) against geocentricity (Earth-centered solar system) which the church had endorsed? That caused a grave crisis involving the credibility of Scripture. Yet, nowhere do we find a didactic portion of Scripture teaching that the Earth is the center of the solar system. To be sure, in narratives, the sun is described as moving across the heavens. That is the way it appeared to ancient people and that is the way it appears today.

I am somewhat amused by the admixture of technical jargon and phenomenological language used in our modern world of science. Consider the nightly weather report. In our town it is no longer a weather report but a meteorological survey. In this survey I become dazzled by the charts and maps and technological nomenclature used by the weatherman. I hear about high pressure centers and aeronautical perturbations and vortices. I learn of the wind velocity and the barometric pressure. The prediction for the morrow is given in terms of precipitation probability quotients. Then, at the end of the survey, the man says, "Sunrise tomorrow will be at 6:45 A.M." I am astonished. Should I phone the T.V. station and protest this blatant conspiracy to reconstruct geocentricity?

Shall I protest the fraudulence and errancy of the report because the weatherman speaks of the sun rising? What is happening here? When we still speak of the sun setting and the sun rising, we are speaking according to appearances and no one calls us liars. Can you imagine reading narrative portions of 2 Chronicles containing descriptions of the external world in terms of barometric pressure and precipitation probability quotients? If we read the narratives of the Bible as if they were scientific textbooks, we are in big trouble.

This is not to say that there are no didactic portions of Scripture that do touch heavily on matters of science. Indeed there are, and in these we often find real conflicts in matters of psychology and biological theories of the nature and origin of man. But many other conflicts would never arise if we recognized the character of phenomenological language in narratives.

Rule 4: The Implicit Is to Be Interpreted by the Explicit

In the business of language we make distinctions between that which is implicit and that which is explicit. Often the difference is a matter of degree and the distinction can be muddled. But usually we can determine the difference between what is actually said and what is left unsaid though implied. I am convinced that if this one rule were consistently followed by Christian communities, the vast majority of doctrinal differences that divide us would be resolved. It is at the point of confusing the implicit and the explicit that it is easy to be careless.

I have read numerous references to the state of angelic beings as being sexless. Where does the Bible say that the angels are sexless? The passage that is always used to support such a contention is Mark 12:25. Here Jesus says that in heaven there will be no marrying or giving in marriage, but we will be like the angels. That implies that angels do not marry, but does it also imply that they are sexless? Does it mean we will be sexless in heaven? It may well be that angels are in fact sexless and that that is the reason they do not marry, but the Bible does not say that. Is it not possible that angels could remain unmarried for other reasons than that they are sexless? The inference of angelic sexlessness is a possible inference from the text but not a *necessary* inference. There is much concerning the biblical teaching of the nature of man as male and female that would strongly suggest that our sexuality will be redeemed but not annihilated.

Another example of less than careful treatment of implications may be seen in the question of the nature of Jesus' resurrection body. Again, I have seen descriptions of Jesus' glorified body as being a body that has the capacity to move unimpeded through solid objects. The biblical warrant for such a claim is found in John 20:19: "When therefore it was evening, on that day, the first *day* of the week, and when the

doors were shut where the disciples were, for fear of the
Jews, Jesus came and stood in their midst, and said to them,
'Peace *be* with you.' " Look carefully at the words of the text.
Does it say that Jesus "dematerialized" and floated through
the door? No, it says that the doors were shut and Jesus came
and stood in their midst. Why does the author mention that
the door was shut? Perhaps to indicate the amazing way
Jesus appeared. Or perhaps merely to accentuate what he
actually says, that the disciples were afraid of the Jews. Is it
possible that Jesus came to his frightened disciples who were
huddled together behind closed doors, opened the door,
walked in and began speaking with them? Again, maybe
Jesus did in fact float through the door, but the text does not
say that. To construct a view of Jesus' resurrected body on
the basis of this text involves unwarranted speculation and
careless exegesis.

That too much can be read into implications is obvious.
This is so easy to do that even the most careful scholars can
fall into it. One of the most precise confessional statements
ever written is the Westminster Confession of Faith. The
care and caution displayed by the Westminster divines in
the drafting of the document was extraordinary. Yet in the
original document there is a glaring example of drawing too
much from an implication. The confession says that we
ought not to pray for persons who have committed the sin
unto death, citing 1 John 5:16. The text reads, "If any man
see his brother sin a sin which is not unto death, he shall ask,
and he shall give him life for them that sin not unto death.
There is a sin unto death: I do not say that he shall pray for
it" (KJV).

In this text John exhorts his readers to pray for brothers
whose sins are not unto death. He does not forbid praying for
those who have committed the sin unto death. He says, "I do
not say that he shall pray for it." That is different from saying, "I say that he shall not pray for it." The former statement is merely the absence of command; the latter is a positive prohibition. Thus if trained scholars meeting in solemn
assembly in a joint effort of exegesis can miss a subtle point

like this, how much more careful should we be when dealing with the text alone?

Not only do we have problems when we draw too many implications from the Scripture, but we also face the problem of squaring implications with what is explicitly taught. When an implication is drawn that is contradictory to what is explicitly stated, the implication must be rejected.

In the perennial debate between Calvinists and Arminians the issues rage back and forth between the camps. Without trying to engage in a full-blown discussion of these issues, let me illustrate the problem of the explicit and the implicit by one recurring problem. With regard to the question of fallen man's moral ability to turn himself to Christ, unaided by the power of the Holy Spirit, many argue that it is within the natural power of man to incline himself to Christ. Countless passages, such as "Whoever believes may in Him have eternal life" (Jn. 3:15), are quoted in the debate. If the Bible says "whoever believes," does that not imply that anybody can believe and respond to Christ on his own? Doesn't the "whoever" imply universal moral ability?

Such passages may suggest an implication of universal ability, but such implications must be rejected if they conflict with an explicit teaching.

Let us begin our analysis of such passages by confining ourselves to what is actually and explicitly said: "Whoever believes may in Him have eternal life." This verse teaches explicitly that all those in the category of believers (A) will be in the category of those having eternal life (B). All A will be B. But what does it say about who will believe; who will be in the category A? It says absolutely nothing. Nothing is said about what it takes to believe or about who will or who will not believe. Elsewhere in Scripture we read, "No one can come to Me, unless it has been granted him from the Father" (Jn. 6:65). This passage does say something explicitly about man's ability to come to Christ. The statement is a universal negative statement with an exceptive clause added. That is, the passage plainly states that no one can (is able) to come to Christ; the exceptive clause says, *unless* it has been granted to him by the Father. This verse explicitly teaches that a necessary prerequisite must take place before a person is able to come to Christ. That prerequisite is that it must be "granted him from the Father." Again, the point is not to settle the controversy between the Calvinist and the Arminian but rather to show that on this point implications cannot be used to cancel explicit teaching.

Implications drawn from comparative statements are also problematic. Let us look at a famous passage from 1 Corinthians that has caused many to stumble. Paul says regarding the virtues of celibacy and marriage, "So then both he who gives his own virgin *daughter* in marriage does well, and he who does not give her in marriage will do better" (1 Cor. 7:38). How many times have you heard it said that Paul was opposed to marriage or that he said marriage was bad? Is that what he in fact says? Obviously not. He makes a comparison between the good and the better, not between the good and the bad. If one thing is said to be better than another, that does not imply that one is good and the other is evil. There are comparative levels of goodness.

The same problem of comparative values came up in the tongues-speaking issue of the sixties. Paul says, "One who speaks in a tongue edifies himself; but one who prophesies edifies the church. Now I wish that you all spoke in tongues, but *even* more that you would prophesy; and greater is one who prophesies than one who speaks in tongues, unless he interprets, so that the church may receive edifying" (1 Cor. 14:4-5). I have heard both sides of the tongues debate distort this passage. Those opposed to tongues have heard Paul say here that prophecy is good and tongues are bad. Again, they missed the point of a comparison of the good and the better. I have heard those in favor of tongues speak as if they were more important than prophecy.

Closely related to the rule of interpreting the implicit by the explicit is the correlate rule to interpret the obscure in the light of the clear. If we interpret the clear in the light of the obscure, we drift into a kind of esoteric interpretation that is inevitably cultic. The basic rule is the rule of care:

careful reading of what the text is actually saying will save us from much confusion and distortion. No great knowledge of logic is necessary, just the simple application of common sense. Sometimes the heat of the controversy causes us to lose that common sense.

Rule 5: Determine Carefully the Meaning of Words

Whatever else the Bible is, it is a book which communicates information verbally. That means that it is filled with words. Thoughts are expressed through the relationship of those words. Each individual word contributes something to the whole of the content expressed. The better we understand the individual words used in biblical statements, the better we will be able to understand the total message of Scripture.

Accurate communication and clear understanding are difficult when words are used imprecisely or ambiguously. Misuse of words and misunderstanding go hand in hand. We have all experienced the frustration of trying to communicate something to someone but not being able to find the right combination of words to make ourselves clear. We have also experienced the frustration of being misunderstood when we have used words properly but our hearers had a misunderstanding of what the words meant.

Laymen often complain that theologians use too many big words. Technical jargon is often baffling and irritating. Technical terms can be used not so much to communicate more accurately but to guard our statements from being too easily understood or to impress people with our vast knowledge. On the other hand, scholars tend to develop a technical language within their field for the sake of precision not confusion. Our everyday language is used in such a broad way that our words take on meanings too elastic to be useful in precise communication.

We can see the advantage of technical language in the medical field even though we are sometimes annoyed with it. If I become ill and say to the doctor, "I don't feel well," he will immediately ask me to be a bit more specific. If he gives me a complete physical examination and says to me, "Your problem is a stomach disorder," I am going to want *him* to be more specific. There are all kinds of stomach problems ranging from mild indigestion to incurable cancer. In medicine, being specific and technical is what saves lives.

If we want to be understood, we must learn to say what we mean and mean what we say. I once heard a theologian giving a lecture in Reformed theology. Part way through his lecture a student raised his hand and said to him, "Sir, should we assume as we are listening to you that you are a Calvinist?" The scholar replied, "Yes, indeed I am," and returned to his lecture. A few moments later he stopped in the middle of a sentence with a sudden look of understanding in his eyes and turned his attention back to the student who had asked the question. He said, "What do you understand a Calvinist to be?" The student answered, "A Calvinist is someone who believes that God brings some people kicking and screaming against their will into his kingdom while excluding others who desperately want in." With that the lecturer's mouth dropped open with shock and he said, "Well in that case, please do not assume I am a Calvinist." If the professor had not asked the student what he understood by the term, the man would have communicated something radically different than he intended because of the student's gross misunderstanding of the words he used. This kind of thing can happen and does happen when we study the Bible.

Probably the greatest advance in biblical scholarship that we have seen in the twentieth century has been in the area of lexicography. That is, we have greatly increased our understanding of the meaning of words found in the Bible. I think the most valuable exegetical tool we have at present is Kittel's *Theological Dictionary of the New Testament.* This series of word studies comprises several large volumes, each costing about $25, and as a reference work it is well worth it. It comprises a series of careful studies of the meanings of key words found in the New Testament. For example a word like *justify* might be examined in a particular volume. The word is subjected to an exhaustive analysis in every known text in which it appears. Its meaning is traced through the period of Homer and classical Greece, its corresponding usage in the Old Testament Greek translation (the Septuagint), its use in the Gospels, in the Epistles and in early church history. Now a student of the Bible, instead of looking up a word in a normal lexicon where he might find a sentence or two of definition with corresponding synonyms, can go to Kittel and find forty or fifty pages of detailed explanation and delineation of all the uses and subtle nuances of the word. We can find out how Plato, Euripides, Luke and Paul used a particular word. This greatly sharpens our understanding of biblical language and also facilitates the accuracy of modern translations of the Bible.

There are usually two basic methods by which words are defined: by etymology and by customary usage. Etymology is the science of word derivations. We see a word like *hippopotamus* and wonder what it means. If we know Greek, we know that the word *hippos* means "horse" and the word *potamos* means "river." Thus we have *hippopotamus* or "river horse." Studying the roots and original meanings of words can be very helpful to gain the flavor of a term. For example, the Hebrew word for *glory* originally meant "heavy" or "weighty." Thus, the glory of God has to do with his "weightiness" or "significance." We do not take him "lightly." But defining words merely in terms of their original meanings can get us into all sorts of trouble.

In addition to origins and derivations, it is extremely important for us to study language in the context of its usage. This is necessary because words undergo changes in meaning depending on how they are used. For example, the word *cute* in the Elizabethan period meant simply bowlegged. When we call a girl cute today, we hope she's not a Shakespearian actress! The word *scan* was defined in English dictionaries within my lifetime as meaning, "to read carefully, in close detail." More recent editions of dictionaries define *scan* as "to skim over lightly." Thus the term has changed its meaning completely over the space of a few years. What happened is that so many people misused the word that its misuse became the "customary meaning." One last example is the word *gay*. A few years ago if a person were called "gay" that meant simply that he was happy.

Words with Multiple Meanings. There are scores of words in the Bible that have multiple meanings. Only the context can determine the particular meaning of a word. For example, the Bible speaks frequently of the will of God. There are at least six different ways this word is used. Sometimes the word *will* refers to the precepts God has revealed to his people. That is, his will is his "prescribed order of duty for his people." The term *will* is also used to describe "God's sovereign action by which God brings to pass whatsoever he wills to happen." We call this God's efficacious will because it effects what he wants. Then there is the sense of *will* being "that which is pleasing to God, that which he delights in."

Let us see how a passage of Scripture could be interpreted in light of these three different meanings of *will*": God is "not willing that any should perish" (2 Pet. 3:9, KJV). This could mean: (1) God has legislated a precept that no one is allowed to perish; it is against the law of God for us to perish; (2) God has sovereignly decreed and effects most certainly that no one will ever perish; or (3) God is not pleased or delighted when people perish. Which of these three would you think is correct? Why? If we examine the context in which this appears and follow the analogy of faith taking into account the larger context of the whole of Scripture, only one of these meanings makes sense, namely, the third.

My favorite example of words with multiple meanings is the word *justify*. In Romans 3:28 Paul says, "For we maintain that a man is justified by faith apart from works of the Law." In James 2:24 we read, "You see that a man is justified by works, and not by faith alone." If the word *justify* means the same thing in both cases, we have an irreconcilable contradiction between two biblical writers on an issue that concerns our eternal destinies. Luther called "justification by faith" the article upon which the church stands or falls. The meaning of justification and the question of how it takes place is no mere trifle. Yet Paul says it is by faith apart from works, and James says it is by works and not by faith alone. To make matters more difficult, Paul insists in Romans 4 that Abraham is justified when he believes the promise of God before he is even circumcised. He has Abraham justified in Genesis 15. James says, "Was not Abraham our father justified by works, when he offered up Isaac his son on the altar?" (Jas. 2:21). James does not have Abraham justified until Genesis 22.

This question of justification is easily resolved if we examine the possible meanings of the term *justify* and apply them within the contexts of the respective passages. The term *justify* may mean (1) to restore to a state of reconciliation with God those who stand under the judgment of his law or (2) to demonstrate or to vindicate.

Jesus says, for example, "Wisdom is justified of all her children" (Lk. 7:35 KJV). What does he mean? Does he mean that wisdom is restored to fellowship with God and saved from his wrath? Obviously not. The plain meaning of his words is that a wise act produces good fruit. The claim to wisdom is vindicated by the result. A wise decision is shown to be wise by its results. Jesus is speaking in practical terms, not theological terms, when he uses the word *justified* in this way.

How does Paul use the word in Romans 3? Here, there is no dispute. Paul is clearly speaking about justification in the ultimate theological sense.

What about James? If we examine the context of James, we will see that he is dealing with a different question from Paul. James says in 2:14, "What use is it, my brethren, if a man says he has faith, but he has no works? Can that faith save him?" James is raising a question of what kind of faith is necessary for salvation. He is saying that true faith brings forth works. A faith without works he calls a dead faith, a faith that is not genuine. The point is that people can say they have faith when in fact they have no faith. The claim to faith is vindicated or justified when it is manifested by the fruit of faith, namely, works. Abraham is justified or vindicated in our sight by his fruit. In a sense, Abraham's claim to justification is justified by his works. The Reformers understood that when they stated the formula, "Justification is by faith alone, but not by a faith that is alone."

Words Whose Meanings Become Doctrinal Concepts. One category of words can give us interpreting fits. It is that group of words that have come to be used for doctrinal concepts. For example, there is the word *save* and the corresponding word *salvation.* In the biblical world, a person was "saved" if he experienced any deliverance from any kind of trouble or calamity. People rescued from military defeat, from bodily injury or disease, from defamation of character or slander all experienced what the Bible calls "salvation." Yet ultimate salvation comes when we are rescued from the power of sin and death and escape the wrath of God. From that specific kind of "saving" we have developed a doctrine of salvation. The problem comes when we come back to the New Testament from which we have extrapolated a doctrine of salvation and read the full-blown ultimate sense of salvation into every text that uses the term salvation. For example, Paul says on one occasion that women will be "saved in childbearing" (1 Tim. 2:15 KJV). Does that mean that there are two ways of salvation? Do men have to be saved through Christ, but women can get into the kingdom of heaven merely by having children? Obviously, Paul is speaking of a different level of salvation when he uses the term with respect to the bearing of children.

Again, we read in 1 Corinthians 7:14: "For the unbelieving husband is sanctified through his wife, and the unbelieving wife is sanctified through her believing husband; for otherwise your children are unclean, but now they are holy." If we consider this passage from the perspective of sanctification, what do we conclude? If sanctification comes after justification and Paul says the unbelieving spouse is sanctified, that can only mean that unbelieving spouses are also justified. This would lead us to a coattail theology: If you don't believe in Christ or want to follow him but are worried that you might be excluded from the kingdom if perchance Jesus is the Son of God, you could hedge your bets, marry a Christian and have the best of both worlds. This would mean that perhaps there are three ways of justification: one is through faith in Christ, another through having children and another through marriage to a believer. This kind of theological confusion would happen if we interpreted the word *sanctify* in its full-blown doctrinal meaning. But the Bible uses the term in other ways. Primarily, *sanctify* means simply "to set apart" or be "consecrated." If two pagans marry and one becomes a Christian, the non-believer is placed in a special relationship to the body of Christ for the sake of the children. That does not mean that they are redeemed.

These examples should be sufficient to show how important it is to gain a careful knowledge of the words employed in Scripture. Countless controversies have developed and heresies born simply by failing to see the multitude of meanings words often have.

Rule 6: Note the Presence of Parallelisms in the Bible

One of the most fascinating characteristics of Hebrew literature is its use of parallelism. Parallelism in ancient Near Eastern languages is common and relatively easy to recognize. The ability to recognize it when it occurs will greatly aid the reader in understanding the text.

Hebrew poetry, like other forms of poetry, is often structured with a particular meter. The metric form, however, is frequently lost in translation. Parallelism is not so easily lost in translation because it involves not so much a rhythm of words and vowels, but a rhythm of thoughts. Parallelism may be defined as a relationship between two or more sentences or clauses that correspond in similarity or are set with each other. There are three basic types of parallelism: synonymous, antithetic and synthetic.

Synonymous parallelism occurs when different lines or parts of a passage present the same thought in a slightly altered manner of expression. For example:

A false witness will not go unpunished,
And he who tells lies will not escape. (Prov. 19:5)
Or:

Come, let us worship and bow down;
Let us kneel before the LORD our Maker. (Ps. 95:6)
Antithetic parallelism occurs when the two parts are set in contrast to each other. They may say the same thing but say it by way of negation.

A wise son accepts his father's discipline,
But a scoffer does not listen to rebuke. (Prov. 13:1)
Or:

Poor is he who works with a negligent hand,
But the hand of the diligent makes rich. (Prov. 10:4)
Synthetic parallelism is a bit more complex than the other forms. Here the first part of the passage creates a sense of expectation which is completed by the second part. It can also move in a progressive, "staircase" movement to a conclusion in a third line.

For, behold, Thine enemies, O LORD,
For, behold, Thine enemies will perish;
All who do iniquity will be scattered. (Ps. 92:9)
Though Jesus didn't speak in poetry, the influence of the form of parallelism can be seen in his words.

Give to him who asks of you, and do
not turn away from him who wants to borrow
from you. (Mt. 5:42)
Or:

Ask, and it shall be given to you;
seek, and you shall find;
knock, and it shall be opened to you. (Mt. 7:7)
The ability to recognize parallelisms can often clear up apparent difficulties in understanding a text. It can also greatly enrich our depth perception of various passages. In the King James Version of the Bible there is a passage that has caused many to stumble. Isaiah 45:6-7 says:

I am the LORD, and there is none else.
I form the light, and create darkness:
I make peace, and create evil:
I the LORD do all these things.
I have been asked about this verse many times. Doesn't it clearly teach that God creates evil? Doesn't this make God

the author of sin? The resolution of this problematic passage
is simple if we recognize the obvious presence of an antithetic parallelism in it. In the first part light is set in contrast
with darkness. In the second part peace is set in contrast
with evil. What is the opposite of peace? The kind of "evil" is
that evil which is contrasted not with goodness but with
"peace." The New American Standard Bible, a recent translation reads, "Causing well-being and creating calamity."
That is a more accurate rendition of this thought expressed
by antithetic parallelism. The point of the passage is that
ultimately God brings the blessing of well-being and peace
to a godly people but visits them with calamity when he acts
in judgment. That is a long way from a notion of being the
creator of evil originally.

Another problematic passage that exhibits a form of parallelism is found in the Lord's prayer. Jesus instructs his disciples to pray, "Do not lead us into temptation" (Mt. 6:13).
James warns us, "Let no one say when he is tempted, 'I am
being tempted by God" (Jas. 1:13). Doesn't Jesus' prayer suggest that God might indeed tempt us, or at least lead us into
temptation? Is Jesus telling us to request that God would not
try to entice us or ensnare us in sin? God forbid.

The problem is easily removed if we examine the other
parts of the parallelism. The passage reads, "Do not lead us
into temptation, but deliver us from evil." This is an example
of synonomous parallelism. The two parts say virtually the
same thing. To be led into temptation is to be exposed to the
onslaught of the evil one. The "temptation" is not the kind
of which James speaks which begins with the inward, in-
ternal inclinations of our own lust, but an external place of
"testing." God does put his people to the test as he did with
Abraham and Jesus in the wilderness.

A further problem with this text is with the translation
of the word *evil*. The noun is in the masculine gender in the
Greek and would be more accurately translated "evil one."
Just "evil in general" would be in the neuter gender. Jesus
is saying, "O Father, put a wall around us, protect us from
Satan. Don't let him get at us. Don't lead us where he can

get us." Again, the initial clue to resolve the passage is found in the parallelism.

The appearance of parallelism can also enrich our understanding of biblical concepts. For example, how did the Hebrew mind understand the notion of blessedness? Hear the words of the classic Hebrew benediction and try to catch a glimpse of their view:

The LORD bless you, and keep you;
The LORD make His face to shine on you,
And be gracious unto you;
The LORD lift up His countenance on you,
And give you peace. (Num. 6:24-26)

By examining the parallel structure of the benediction we are enriched not only by a deeper understanding of blessedness but also of what a Jew means by the full measure of "peace." Note that the terms *peace, grace,* and *keep* are used in a synonomous way. *Peace* means more than the absence of war. It means experiencing the grace of God in being preserved by him. What does being *kept* mean to a people who experience a pilgrim character of life? The history of the Jews is the history of the exile who constantly faces the impermanence of life. To be blessed by the grace of God and to experience peace are related.

But what is blessedness? Note that in the last two parts of the benediction blessedness is replaced by images of beholding the face of God: "The LORD make His face to shine . . . [or] lift up His countenance." For a Jew the ultimate state of blessedness comes from being able to stand so near to God as to see his face. The one thing prohibited fallen man in the Old Testament was to behold the face of God. They could draw near; Moses could view God's back parts; they could have fellowship with God, but his face could not be seen. But the hope of Israel—the final and highest benediction—was the hope of seeing God face to face.

For the Christian our ultimate state of glory is expressed in terms of the beatific vision, the vision of God face to face. Conversely, in Hebrew categories, the notion of the curse of God is expressed in the imagery of God's turning his back—

his looking away. Nearness to God is blessing; absence of God is curse.

Rule 7: Note the Difference between Proverb and Law

A common mistake in biblical interpretation and application is to give a proverbial saying the weight or force of a moral absolute. Proverbs are catchy little couplets designed to express practical truisms. They reflect principles of wisdom for godly living. They do not reflect moral laws that are to be applied absolutely to every conceivable life situation.

To show the problem of making them absolute, let me first illustrate from English proverbs. Remember the famous line, "Look before you leap"? This saying is designed to teach something of the wisdom of considering the consequences of your actions. We ought not to be impetuous, jumping into things before we know what we are doing. What about the other saying, "He who hesitates is lost"? What if we make both sayings absolute? On the one hand, if we hesitate we are lost. But if we are to look before we leap, we must hesitate. The conclusion is, "He who hesitates to look before he leaps is lost!"

The same kind of thing can happen with the biblical proverbs. It can even happen with some of the wisdom sayings of Jesus. Jesus says, "He who is not with Me is against Me" (Mt. 12:30). But Jesus also said, "He who is not against you is for you" (Lk. 9:50). How can both be true? We all know that in some circumstances silence means consent, and in others it indicates hostility. In some cases lack of opposition means support; in other cases lack of support indicates opposition.

Proverbs 26:4-5 illustrates clearly how proverbs can be contradictory if taken as absolutes with no exceptions. Verse 4 says, "Do not answer a fool according to his folly, Lest you also be like him." Verse 5 says, "Answer a fool as his folly deserves, Lest he be wise in his own eyes." Thus, there are times when it is foolish to answer a fool according to his folly, and there are times when it is wise to answer a fool with foolishness.

As we distinguish between proverb and law, we must also distinguish between different forms of laws. The basic two types or forms of law that we find in the Bible are apodictic law and casuistic law. Apodictic law expresses absolutes and follows a direct personal form such as "Thou shalt" or "Thou shalt not." We find this form of law clearly in the Ten Commandments.

Casuistic law is expressed in the "if . . . then" form of conditional statement. This is the basis for the so-called case law. The casuistic form gives a series of "examples" which act as guidelines for rendering justice. This form is similar to our use and concept of precedent in the American legal system. For example, Exodus 23:4 instructs: "If you meet your enemy's ox or his donkey wandering away, you shall surely return it to him." Note that the first clause is casuistic and the second apodictic. Here explicit instructions are given concerning the return of the enemy's ox or donkey. But what if I see my enemy's cow or camel wandering away, do I have to return them? The law doesn't say so. Casuistic law gives the principle by example. It implicitly covers cows, camels, chickens and horses. If the Bible gave an explicit ruling for every conceivable eventuality, we would need huge libraries to contain all the legal volumes necessary. Case law provides the illustration of the principle, but the principle has an obviously wider realm of application.

Rule 8: Observe the Difference between the Spirit and the Letter of the Law

We all know the reputation of the Pharisees in the New Testament who were quite scrupulous about keeping the letter of the law while violating the spirit constantly. There are stories of Israelites who got around the rule of not being able to travel far on the Sabbath day by cleverly stretching their own "Sabbath day journeys." The rabbis ruled that a Sabbath day's journey was limited to a fixed distance measured from one's place of residence. Thus, if a "legalist" wanted to travel a greater distance on the Sabbath than the law allowed, during the week he would have travelers or friends place his toothbrush or some other personal item under a rock at different intervals spaced miles apart. Now the legalist had technically established residency at each place. To travel on the Sabbath, all he had to do was go from "residence" to "residence" picking up his toothbrushes as he went. Here the letter of the law was obeyed, but the spirit of the law was demolished.

There were a variety of types of legalists in New Testament times. The first and most famous was the type that legislated rules and regulations beyond what God had commanded. Jesus rebuked the Pharisees for making the tradition of the rabbis as authoritative as the Law of Moses. Attributing divine authority to human laws is the chief type of legalism. But it is not the only type. The Sabbath day's journey incident illustrates the other most frequently found type. To obey the letter while violating the spirit makes one technically righteous but actually corrupt.

Another way the law is distorted is by trying to obey the spirit of the law but ignoring the letter. Letter and spirit are inseparably related. The legalists destroy the spirit and the antinomian destroys the letter.

Jesus' discussion of the Mosaic Law in the Sermon on the Mount has been woefully abused by interpreters. For example, I recently read a newspaper article written by a prominent psychiatrist in which Jesus' ethical teaching was severly criticized. The psychiatrist said he couldn't understand why Jesus was held in such wide esteem as an ethical teacher since his ethics were so naive, pointing particularly to Jesus' teaching on murder and adultery. The psychiatrist interpreted Jesus' comments on these subjects as equating the severity of murder with anger and adultery with lust. Any teacher who thinks anger is as bad as murder or a lustful thought as bad as adultery has a twisted sense of ethics. He went on to show how much more devastating are the effects of murder and adultery than anger or lust. If a person is angry at someone, that can be harmful. But if the anger leads to murder, the implications are far greater. Anger doesn't take a person's life and leave wives widowed and children fatherless. Murder does. If I have a lustful thought, it may injure the purity of my own mind, but I haven't involved the woman in an act of infidelity to her husband that could destroy her marriage and her home. And so the psychiatrist went on with his analysis saying that such ethical teaching was a serious detriment to responsible living.

At a more popular level of thinking the same misunderstanding of the Sermon on the Mount abounds. Some people argue, "Well, I've already lusted after her (or him). I may as well go ahead and commit adultery since I'm already guilty of the crime in the eyes of God." This is not only a gross distortion of what Jesus said, but it compounds the felony of lust with the full measure of the sin of adultery.

Look at what Jesus says about these matters and see if he is as naive as his critics maintain:

> *You have heard that the ancients were told, "You shall not commit murder" and "Whoever commits murder shall be liable to the court." But I say to you that every one who is angry with his brother shall be guilty before the court; and whoever shall say to his brother, "Raca," shall be guilty before the supreme court; and whoever shall say, "You fool," shall be guilty* enough to go *into the hell of fire. (Mt. 5:21-22)*

Also note:

> *You have heard that it was said, "YOU SHALL NOT COMMIT ADULTERY"; but I say to you, that every one who looks on a woman to lust for her has committed adultery with her already in his heart. (Mt. 5:27-28)*

Nowhere in these passages does Jesus say that anger is as bad as murder or that lust is as bad as adultery. What he does say is that if a person refrains from murder but hates his brother or insults his brother he has not fulfilled the full import of the law against murder. Murder is a sin, but so is hatred and slander.

The point of Jesus' teaching is that the law has a wider application than its letter. If you murder someone you violate the letter of the law; if you hate someone you violate the spirit. He says, "Whoever commits murder shall be liable to the court. . . . Every one who is angry with his brother shall be guilty before the court." That is, all Jesus says is that both anger and murder are sins. Not that they are equal in their damaging results or even that they are equally heinous. He does not even say, as many have inferred, that the punishment of both is equal. To be sure, he says that if you slander a person by calling him a fool, you will be guilty enough to go to hell. That does not, however, carry with it the implication that all punishment in hell is equal. What he says is that slander is a serious enough offense, being destructive to another person's life, that it is worthy of hell. Jesus is underlining the seriousness of all sin. But is punishment in hell the same for every sin? Jesus doesn't teach that. The New Testament warns against "storing up wrath for yourself in the day of wrath" (Rom. 2:5). How can one "store up wrath" if the punishment of sinners in hell is equal? Jesus says that God will judge each man according to his works. Some will be beaten with few stripes and some with many (Lk. 12:47-48). The point is that all sin will be punished, not that the punishment will be the same. The biblical principle of justice does differentiate between degrees of evil and degrees of punishment.

With regard to adultery Jesus says that when lust occurs, a person has committed adultery in his "heart." The point is that, though the letter of the law has been kept, the spirit of the law has been broken; there is more to sin than external acts. God is concerned with the heart as well as with the act. The Pharisees prided themselves in their righteousness deluding themselves into thinking they were keeping the whole law because they kept the letter.

The whole point of Jesus' comments on the law is introduced by the statement:

Do not think that I came to abolish the Law or the Prophets; I did not come to abolish, but to fulfill. For truly I say to you, until heaven and earth pass away, not the smallest letter or stroke shall pass away from the Law, until all is accomplished. Whoever then annuls one of the least of these com-

mandments, and so teaches others, shall be called least in the kingdom of heaven; but whoever keeps and teaches them, he shall be called great in the kingdom of heaven. (Mt. 5:17-19)

This passage teaches clearly that Jesus is concerned with the keeping of the letter of the law. Not merely the letter is important, but the "smallest letter" or "stroke" is to be kept and taught. But Jesus goes beyond the letter to a concern for the spirit. He does not set the spirit over against the letter or substitute the spirit for the letter, but he adds the spirit to the letter. Here is the key: "For I say to you, that unless your righteousness surpasses *that* of the scribes and Pharisees, you shall not enter the kingdom of heaven" (Mt. 5:20). The Pharisees noted the letter; Christians are to note both the letter and the spirit. Jesus makes this a prerequisite for entrance into his kingdom. His comments on murder and adultery follow this injunction and elucidate his principle.

Rule 9: Be Careful with Parables

Of all the various literary forms we find in Scripture, the parable is often considered the easiest to understand and interpret. People usually enjoy sermons that are based on parables. Since parables are concrete stories based on life situations, they seem easier to handle than abstract concepts. Yet, from the viewpoint of the New Testament scholar, the parables present unique difficulties in interpretation.

What is so hard about parables? Why can't these pithy stories be simply presented and expounded? There are several answers to these questions. First is the problem of the original intent of the parable. Jesus was obviously fond of using the parable as a teaching device. The puzzling question, however, is whether he used parables to elucidate his teaching or to obscure it. The debate focuses on Jesus' cryptic words found in Mark 4:10-12:

And as soon as He was alone, His followers, along with the twelve, began *asking Him* about *the parables. And He*

*was saying to them, "To you has been given the mystery of
the kingdom of God; but those who are outside get everything in parables, in order that WHILE SEEING, THEY
MAY SEE AND NOT PERCEIVE; AND WHILE HEARING,
THEY MAY HEAR AND NOT UNDERSTAND LEST THEY
RETURN AGAIN AND BE FORGIVEN."*
Jesus continues by giving a detailed explanation of the Parable of the Sower to his disciples. What does he mean by saying that the parables are not to be perceived by those who
have not been given the secret of the kingdom of God? Some
translators are so offended by this saying that they have
actually changed the wording of the text to avoid the problem. Such textual manipulation has no literary justification. Others see in these words an allusion to the judgment
of God upon the hardened hearts of Israel and is an echo of
God's commission to the prophet Isaiah. In Isaiah's famous
vision in the temple (Is. 6:8-13) God said to him, "Whom
shall I send, and who will go for Us?" Isaiah volunteered by
saying, "Here am I. Send me!" God responded to Isaiah's
words by saying,
Go, and tell this people:
"Keep on listening, but do not perceive;
Keep on looking, but do not understand."
Render the hearts of this people insensitive,
Their ears dull,
And their eyes dim,
Lest they see with their eyes,
Hear with their ears,
Understand with their hearts,
And repent and be healed.
Here God's judgment involves giving the people "fat hearts"
as a judgment on their sin. It is punishment in kind. The
people did not want to listen to God, so he took away their
capacity to hear him.

Jesus frequently uses the words, "He that has ears to hear,
let him hear." The way Jesus uses this phrase strongly suggests that not everyone who is "hearing" his words is hearing them in the special sense that he intends.

If Jesus is to be taken seriously about the use of parables, we must acknowledge an element of concealment in them. But that is not to say that the only purpose of a parable is to obscure or conceal the mystery of the kingdom to the impenitent. A parable is not a riddle. It was meant to be understood, at least by those who were open to it. There is also the consideration that Jesus' enemies did have some understanding of the parables. At least enough to be infuriated by them.

In dealing with the "concealment" aspect of the parables there is one very important factor to keep in mind. The parables were originally given to an audience that lived before the cross and the resurrection. At that point in time people did not have the benefit of the entire New Testament as a background to aid them in interpreting the parables. Much of the parabolic material concerns the kingdom of God. At the time the parables were given there was much popular misconception of the meaning of the kingdom in the minds of Jesus' hearers. Thus, the parables were not always easy to understand. Even the disciples had to ask Jesus for a more detailed interpretation of them.

Another problem in interpreting parables rests with the question of the relationship of parable to allegory. When Jesus does interpret the Parable of the Sower, he does so in allegorical fashion. That might lead us to assume that all the parables have an allegorical meaning with each detail having a specific "spiritual" meaning. If we approach the parables in this way, we will get ourselves into trouble. If we treat all the parables as allegory, we will soon discover that the teaching of Jesus becomes a mass of confusion. Many of the parables are simply not suited to allegorical interpretation. It may be fun, especially in preaching, to allow our imaginations to roam freely seeking the allegorical meaning of the details of the parables, but it will not be very instructive.

The safest and probably most accurate way to treat the parables is to look for one basic central point in them. As a rule of thumb, I avoid all allegorizing of the parables except where the New Testament clearly indicates an allegorical meaning. Some parables, such as The Prodigal Son, obviously have more than one point. Some are extended similes; others are comparative stories; others have an obvious moral application. Even my rule of thumb of "one central meaning" cannot be rigidly applied. Again, the basic rule is one of care in dealing with them. Here is where consultation of several commentaries will be exceedingly helpful and usually necessary.

Rule 10: Be Careful with Predictive Prophecy

Handling predictive prophecy both from the New Testament and the Old is one of the most abused forms of biblical interpretation. Interpretations range from the skeptical, naturalistic method which virtually eliminates predictive prophecy to the wild, bizarre method that sees in every contemporary event a "clear" fulfillment of a biblical prophecy.

Higher critical methods have sometimes worked on the assumption that anything that smacks of future prediction and fulfillment of prophecy indicates a later interpolation in the text. The tacit assumption is that future prediction with accurate results is impossible. Thus any occurrence of this must indicate that the prediction was written or inserted at a date later than the "fulfillment." This involves theological "weaseling" and should not be taken seriously. The problem is "prejudice" in the classical meaning of the term; the text is "pre-judged" on the basis of gratuitous assumptions.

On the other hand, some conservative thinkers insist that every detail of biblical prophecy must be fulfilled to the letter, leaving no room for symbolic predictions or predictions that have a broader scope of meaning.

If we examine how the New Testament treats Old Testament prophecy, we discover that in some cases an appeal is made to fulfillment of the letter (such as the birth of the Messiah in Bethlehem) and fulfillment in a broader scope (such as the fulfillment of Malachi's prophecy of the return of Elijah).

Let us examine the Malachi prophecy and the way it is

handled in the New Testament to gain a glimpse of the complexity of the problem of prophecy. In the last chapter of the Old Testament we read the following:

Behold, I am going to send you Elijah the prophet before the coming of the great and terrible day of the LORD. And he will restore the hearts of the fathers to their children, and the hearts of children to their fathers, lest I come and smite the land with a curse. (Mal. 4:5-6)

With this prophecy of the return of Elijah the Old Testament ends. For four hundred years afterwards there is no voice of prophecy in the land of Israel. Then suddenly John the Baptist appears on the scene. Speculation runs rampant as to his identity. In John's Gospel we read that the Jews sent a delegation of priests and Levites from Jerusalem to inquire of John's identity (Jn. 1:19-28). First they asked, "Are you the Messiah?" And John responded in the negative. The next question they asked was, "Are you Elijah?" John's answer was unequivocable, "I am not."

The problem of the relationship of John the Baptist to Elijah is compounded by Jesus' words on the matter in Mark 9:12-13:

Elijah does first come and restore everything. And yet how is it written of the Son of Man that He should suffer many things and be treated with contempt? But I say to you, that Elijah has indeed come, and they did to him whatever they wished, just as it is written of him.

Again, Jesus says in Matthew 11:13-15: "For all the prophets and the Law prophesied until John. And if you care to accept *it*, he himself is Elijah, who was to come. He who has ears to hear, let him hear."

Thus, we have John the Baptist saying plainly that he is not Elijah and Jesus saying that he is. But note how Jesus made that statement. He qualified it by prefacing his words with "if you care to accept it." Obviously Jesus had something somewhat cryptic in mind. Perhaps the answer to the riddle may be found in the annunciation of John's birth by the angel Gabriel: "And it is he who will go *as a forerunner* before Him in the spirit and power of Elijah" (Lk. 1:17).

The puzzle may be solved by pointing out that John was not actually the reincarnation or reappearance of Elijah himself. But in a certain sense he was Elijah; he came in the spirit and power of Elijah. This would explain Jesus' cryptic preface as well as John's denial. The significant point, however, is the way Jesus dealt with the Old Testament prophecy. At least in this case Jesus gave some latitude to fulfillment and did not insist upon the actual identity of Elijah and John the Baptist.

Of all forms of prophecy the apocalyptic form is the most difficult to handle. Apocalyptic literature is characterized by a high degree of symbolic imagery that is sometimes interpreted for us and sometimes left uninterpreted. The three most prominent books that fit this category are Daniel, Ezekiel and Revelation. It is very easy to get bewildered with Daniel's symbols and the drama of the New Testament apocalypse. One important key to interpreting these images is to seek the general meaning of such images in the Bible itself. For example, most of the images of the book of Revelation are found elsewhere in the Bible, particularly in the Old Testament.

Interpreting prophecy can be so complex that giving any detailed formula to follow is well beyond the scope of this book. The student of Scripture would do well to make a special study of this category of biblical literature. Again, the general emphasis is on care. We must approach prophecy very carefully with a sober attitude. If we do so, the results of studying the prophetic books are rewarding.

These practical rules for interpretation do not cover every technical problem that we encounter in Scripture. They are aids and guidelines for our study. They offer no magic formula for perfect success in understanding each text of the Bible. But they do offer help not only in recognizing special problems in the Bible but in resolving them as well. If we adopt these basic guidelines, we will save ourselves many perplexing hours of confusion.

5

Culture & the Bible

When Herman Melville wrote his novel *Redburn,* he told the story of a young man who went to sea for the first time. When he left for England, Redburn's father gave him a very old map of the city of Liverpool. After the arduous voyage, Redburn entered Liverpool confident that his father's map would guide him through the city. But the map failed him. Too many changes had taken place since the map was made. Old landmarks had disappeared, streets had changed their names and people's residences were gone.

Some see in the story of Redburn Melville's private protest at the inadequacy of the ancient Scriptures to guide him through life. That same sense of protest that grows out of frustration is being made by many people today.

Cultural Conditioning and the Bible
One burning issue in the Christian world rages over the question of the sense and degree to which the Bible is conditioned by culture. Was the Bible written for first-century

Christians only? Or was it written for people of all eras? We might be quick to answer according to the latter, but can we say that without reservation? Is there any part of Scripture that is bound by its cultural setting and thus limited in its application to its own cultural setting?

Unless we maintain that the Bible fell down from heaven on a parachute, inscribed by a celestial pen in a peculiar heavenly language uniquely suited as a vehicle for divine revelation, or that the Bible was dictated directly and immediately by God without reference to any local custom, style or perspective, we are going to have to face the culture gap. That is, the Bible reflects the culture of its day. The question then is, how can it have authority over us in our day?

An ecclesiastical controversy in the sixties illustrates the problem of culture. In 1967 the United Presbyterian Church in the U. S. A. adopted a new confession with the following statement concerning the Bible:

The Scriptures, given under the guidance of the Holy Spirit, are nevertheless the words of men, conditioned by the language, thought forms, and literary fashions of the places and times at which they were written. They reflect views of life, history, and the cosmos which were then current. The church therefore, has an obligation to approach the Scriptures with literary and historical understanding. As God has spoken his word in diverse cultural situations, the church is confident that he will continue to speak through the Scriptures in a changing world and in every form of human culture.

These words of the Confession of 1967 engendered a great deal of dialogue, debate and controversy during the decade of the sixties. The debate was centered not so much on what the confession said but on what it left unsaid. Unfortunately the confession did not spell out in detail what was meant by each statement. A great deal of latitude for drawing implications and inferences was left. Considering the statement merely in terms of what the words explicitly state, either the orthodox B. B. Warfield or the existentialist Rudolf Bultmann could assent to it. How much authority would be seen in Scripture would depend largely on how one understood the word *conditioned* in the creed. At the time of the debate many conservatives manifested great distress to think that the Bible was "conditioned" in any sense by ancient culture. Many liberals argued that Scripture was not only "conditioned" by culture but was "bound" by it.

In addition to the question of the sense and degree of "conditioning" of culture on the Bible is the question of the sense and degree by which the Scriptures "reflect views of life, history, and the cosmos" of antiquity. Does *reflect* mean that the Bible teaches as true, outmoded and incorrect views of life, history and cosmos? Is this cultural perspective part of the essence of the message of Scripture? Or does *reflect* mean that we can read between the lines of Scripture noting such things as phenomenal language and see a cultural setting in which a culture-transcending message is given? How we answer these questions reveals a great deal about our overall view of Scripture. Again, the nature of Scripture will affect our interpretation of it. The ultimate issue here is this: to what extent is the Bible's relevance and authority limited by changing human structures and perspectives in the biblical text?

As we have already seen, in order to produce an accurate exegesis of a biblical text and understand what was said and what was meant, a student must be involved with questions of language (Greek, Hebrew, Aramaic), style, syntax, historical and geographical context, author, destination and literary genre. This kind of analysis is necessary for interpreting any body of literature—even contemporary literature.

In a word, the better I understand the first-century culture of Palestine, the easier it becomes for me to have an accurate understanding of what was being said. But the Bible was written a long time ago, in a cultural setting quite different from our own, and it is not always easy to bridge the sheer chasm of time between the first century and the twentieth century.

Cultural Conditioning and the Reader

The problem becomes more acute when I realize that not only is the Bible conditioned by its cultural setting, but I am conditioned by my cultural setting as well. It often becomes difficult for me to hear and understand what the Bible is saying because I bring to it a host of extra-biblical assumptions. This is probably the biggest problem of "cultural conditioning" we face. No one of us ever totally escapes being a child of our age. I am sure that I am holding and teaching views that have nothing to do with Christian thought but are intrusions into my mind from my own background. If I knew which of my ideas were out of harmony with Scripture, I would try to change them. But sorting out my own views is not always easy. All of us are prone to making the same mistakes over and over again. Our blindspots are so called because we are oblivious to them.

The problem of subjective blindspots was brought home to me in an experience with a do-it-yourself stereo building kit project. I purchased such a kit and asked a friend who is an expert in electronics to help me build it. As I read the directions, he carefully wired the components in a series of over two hundred steps. When we were finished, we plugged it in and sat back to enjoy the music. What we heard was out of this world. In fact it sounded more like Venusian music than anything conceived on this earth! The weird cacophony of noise made it quite evident that we had made a mistake.

Painstakingly, we retraced our tracks. We went over the schematic and the instruction checklist a total of eight times. We found no error. Finally in desperation, we decided to reverse our roles. This time my friend read the instructions, and I (a complete novice) checked the wiring points. At about point 134 I found the error. A wire had been soldered to the wrong terminal. What happened? My friend the expert made a mistake in wiring the first time. He made the same mistake eight more times. Chances are that his mistaken perspective would have made him blind to the error again and again.

That is how we often come to Scripture. This is one reason why we must temper our zeal in criticizing Scripture by allowing Scripture to criticize us: we need to become aware that the perspective we bring to the Word may well be a distortion of truth.

I am convinced that the problem of the influence of the twentieth-century secular mindset is a far more formidable obstacle to accurate biblical interpretation than is the problem of the conditioning of ancient culture. This is one of the basic reasons the Reformers sought to approach exegesis in terms of the *tabula rasa* ideal. The interpreter was expected to strive as hard as possible for an objective reading of the text through the grammatico-historical approach. Though subjective influences always present a clear and present danger of distortion, the student of the Bible was expected to utilize every possible safeguard in the pursuit of the ideal, listening to the message of Scripture without mixing in his own prejudices.

In recent years new approaches to biblical interpretation have been vying for acceptance. One of the most significant of these approaches is the "existential method." The existential method has sharply departed from the classical method by means of a new hermeneutic. Bultmann, for example, not only maintains that the *tabula rasa* approach is unattainable but insists that it is undesirable. Because the Bible was written in a prescientific age and is substantially the result of the formative influence of the life situation of the early Christian community, it must be modernized before it can be relevant to us. Bultmann calls for a necessary "prior understanding" before we can come to the text at all. If modern man is to get any valid answers to his questions from the Bible, he must first come to the Bible with the right questions. Those questions can only be provided by a proper philosophical understanding of human existence. Such an understanding, however, is not to be gleaned from Scripture but must be formulated prior to coming to Scripture.

Here the twentieth-century mindset blatantly conditions and binds the first-century texts. (Bultmann finds his own prior understanding, within the broad framework of Martin Heidegger's existential or phenomenological philosophy.) The net result is a method that moves inexorably toward a subjective Bible removed from its own history. Here the first-century message is swallowed up and absorbed by the twentieth-century mentality.

Even if biblical interpreters can agree on a method of exegesis and can even agree on the exegesis itself, we are still left with the questions of application, relevance and obligation imposed by the text. If we agree that the Bible is inspired by God and not merely the product of prescientific authors, we are still faced with questions of application. Does what the Bible commands first-century Christians to do apply to us? In what sense do the Scriptures bind our consciences today?

Principle and Custom
In many circles today the issue is principle and custom. Unless we conclude that all of Scripture is principle and thus binding on all people of all ages, or that all Scripture is local custom with no relevance beyond its immediate historical context, we are forced to establish some categories and guidelines for discerning the difference.

To illustrate the problem let us see what happens when we hold that everything in Scripture is principle and nothing merely a reflection of local custom. If that is the case, then some radical changes must be made in evangelism if we are going to be obedient to Scripture. Jesus says, "Carry no purse, no bag, no shoes; and greet no one on the way" (Lk. 10:4). If we make this text a transcultural principle, then it is time for Billy Graham to start preaching in his bare feet! Obviously, the point of this text is not to set down a perennial requirement of barefooted evangelism.

Other matters, however, are not so obvious. Christians remain divided, for example, on the foot-washing rite. Is this a perpetual mandate for the church of all ages or a local custom illustrating a principle of humble servanthood? Does the principle remain and the custom vanish in a shoe-wearing culture? Or does the custom remain with the principle regardless of foot apparel?

To see the complexities of the dilemma, let us examine the famous "hair-covering" passage of 1 Corinthians 11. The Revised Standard Version translates this to require a woman to cover her head with a veil when she prophesies. In applying this command to our culture we are faced with four distinct options:

1. It is entirely custom. The whole passage reflects a cultural custom that has no relevance today. The veil is local customary headgear; the uncovering of the head reflects a local sign of prostitution. The sign of the woman subordinating herself to the man is a Jewish custom that is outmoded in light of the overall teaching of the New Testament. Since we live in a different culture, it is no longer necessary for a woman to cover her head with a veil; it is no longer necessary for a woman to cover her head with anything; it is no longer necessary for a woman to be subordinate to a man.

2. It is entirely principle. In this case everything in the passage is regarded as culturally transcending principle. That would mean by way of application that (a) Women must be submissive to men during prayer; (b) Women must always give a sign of that submission by covering their heads; (c) Women must cover their heads with a veil as the only appropriate sign.

3. It is partly principle–partly custom (Option A). In this approach, part of the passage is regarded as principle and thus binding for all generations, and part is seen as custom that is no longer binding. The principle of female submission is transcultural, but the means of expressing it (covering the head with a veil) is customary and may be changed.

4. It is partly principle (Option B). In this final option the principle of female submission and the symbolic act of covering the head are to be perpetual. The article of covering may vary from culture to culture. A veil may be replaced by a babushka or a hat.

Which of these alternatives would be most pleasing to God? I certainly do not know the final answer to the question. Questions like these are usually exceedingly complex and do not yield to simplistic solutions. One thing is clear, however. We need some kind of practical guidelines to aid us in unraveling such problems. These questions are frequently of a type that require some sort of active decision and cannot be put on the theological back burner for future generations to figure out. The following practical guidelines should help us.

Practical Guidelines

1. Examine the Bible itself for apparent areas of custom. By close scrutiny of the Scriptures themselves we can see that they display a certain latitude of custom. For example, divine principles from the Old Testament culture have been restated in a New Testament culture. By seeing Old Testament laws and principles restated in the New Testament, we see that some common core of principle transcends custom, culture and social convention. At the same time, we see some Old Testament principles (such as the dietary laws of the Pentateuch) abrogated in the New Testament. This is not to say that the dietary laws of the Old Testament were merely matters of Jewish custom. But we see a difference in the redemptive-historical situation in which Christ abrogates the old law. What we must be careful to note is that neither the idea of carrying all Old Testament principles over to the New Testament nor carrying none of them over can be justified by the Bible itself.

What kind of cultural customs are capable of reacculturation? Language is one obvious factor of cultural fluidity. The Old Testament laws were capable of being translated from Hebrew into Greek. This matter gives us at least a clue to the variable nature of verbal communication. That is, language is a cultural aspect that is open to change; not that the biblical content may be distorted linguistically, but that the gospel can be preached in English as well as Greek.

Second, we see that Old Testament styles of dress are not fixed perpetually for God's people. Principles of modesty prevail, but local styles of dress may change. The Old Testament does not prescribe a godly uniform that must be worn by believers of all ages. Other normal cultural differences such as monetary systems are clearly open to change. Christians are not obligated to use the denarius instead of the dollar.

Such an analysis of cultural modes of expression may be simple with respect to clothes and money, but matters of cultural institutions are more difficult. For example, slavery has often been introduced into modern controversies over civil obedience as well as debates concerning marital structures of authority. In the same context that Paul calls women to be submissive to husbands he calls slaves to be submissive to their masters. Some have argued that since the seeds of the abolition of slavery are sown in the New Testament, so also are the seeds of the abolition of female subordination. Both represent institutional structures that are culturally conditioned, according to this line of reasoning.

Here we must be careful to distinguish between institutions the Bible merely recognizes as existing, such as "the powers that be" (Rom. 13:1, KJV), and those which the Bible positively institutes, endorses and ordains. The principle of submission to existing authority structures (such as the Roman government) does not carry with it a necessary implication of God's endorsement of those structures but merely a call to humility and civil obedience. God, in his ultimate secret providence may ordain that there be a Caesar Augustus without endorsing Caesar as a model of Christian virtue. Yet, the institution of the structures and authority patterns of marriage are given in the context of positive institution and endorsement in both Testaments. To put the biblical structures of the home on a par with the slavery question is to obscure the many differences between the two. Thus, the Scriptures provide a basis for Christian behavior in the midst of oppressive or evil situations as well as ordaining structures that are to mirror the good designs of creation.

2. *Allow for Christian distinctives in the first century.* It

is one thing to seek a more lucid understanding of the biblical content by investigating the cultural situation of the first century; it is quite another to interpret the New Testament as if it were merely an echo of the first-century culture. To do so would be to fail to account for the serious conflict the church experienced as it confronted the first-century world. Christians were not thrown to the lions for their penchant for conformity.

Some very subtle means of relativizing the text occur when we read into the text cultural considerations that ought not to be there. For example, with respect to the hair-covering issue in Corinth, numerous commentators on the Epistle point out that the local sign of the prostitute in Corinth was the uncovered head. Therefore, the argument runs, the reason why Paul wanted women to cover their heads was to avoid a scandalous appearance of Christian women in the external guise of prostitutes.

What is wrong with this kind of speculation? The basic problem here is that our reconstructed knowledge of first-century Corinth has led us to supply Paul with a rationale that is foreign to the one he gives himself. In a word, we are not only putting words into the apostle's mouth, but we are ignoring words that are there. If Paul merely told women in Corinth to cover their heads and gave no rationale for such instruction, we would be strongly inclined to supply it via our cultural knowledge. In this case, however, Paul provides a rationale which is based on an appeal to creation not to the custom of Corinthian harlots. We must be careful not to let our zeal for knowledge of the culture obscure what is actually said. To subordinate Paul's stated reason to our speculatively conceived reason is to slander the apostle and turn exegesis into eisegesis.

3. The creation ordinances are indicators of the transcultural principle. If any biblical principles transcend local customary limits, they are the appeals drawn from creation. Appeals to creation ordinances reflect stipulations a covenant God makes with man *qua* man. The laws of creation are not given to man as Hebrew or man as Christian or man as Corinthian, but are rooted in basic human responsibility to God. To set principles of creation aside as mere local custom is the worst kind of relativizing and dehistoricizing of the biblical content. Yet it is precisely at this point that many scholars have relativized scriptural principles. Here we see the existential method operating most blatantly. To illustrate the importance of creation ordinances we can examine Jesus' treatment of divorce. When the Pharisees tested Jesus by asking if divorce were lawful for any cause, Jesus responded by citing the creation ordinance of marriage: "Have you not read, that He who created *them* from the beginning MADE THEM MALE AND FEMALE, and said, 'FOR THIS CAUSE A MAN SHALL LEAVE...'? What therefore God has joined together, let no man separate" (Mt. 19:4-6).

By reconstructing the life situation of this narrative, it is easy to see that the test of the Pharisees involved getting Jesus' opinion on an issue which sharply divided the rabbinic schools of Shammai and Hillel. Rather than siding with either side completely, Jesus took the matter back to creation to get the norms of marriage in perspective. To be sure, he acknowledged the Mosaic modification of the law of creation, but he refused to weaken the norm further by yielding to public pressure or the cultural opinions of his contemporaries. The inference to be drawn is that the creation ordinances are normative unless explicitly modified by later biblical revelation.

4. In areas of uncertainty use the principle of humility. What if, after careful consideration of a biblical mandate, we remain uncertain as to its character as principle or custom? If we must decide to treat it one way or the other but have no conclusive means to make the decision, what can we do? Here the biblical principle of humility can be helpful. The issue is simple. Would it be better to treat a possible custom as a principle and be guilty of being overscrupulous in our design to obey God? Or would it be better to treat a possible principle as a custom and be guilty of being unscrupulous in demoting a transcendent requirement of God to the level of a mere human convention? I hope the answer is obvious.

If the principle of humility is isolated from the other guidelines mentioned, it can easily be misconstrued as a basis for legalism. We do not have the right to legislate the consciences of Christians where God has left them free. It cannot be applied in an absolutistic way where Scripture is silent. The principle applies where we have biblical mandates whose nature remains uncertain (as to custom and principle) after all the arduous labor of exegesis has been exhausted.

To short-circuit such labor by a blanket scrupulosity would obscure the distinction between custom and principle. This is a guideline of last resort and would be destructive if used as a first resort.

The problem of cultural conditioning is a real one. Barriers of time, place and language frequently make communication difficult. Still, the barriers of culture are not so severe as to drive us to skepticism or despair of understanding God's Word. It is comforting that this Book has indeed manifested a peculiar ability to speak to the deepest needs and communicate the gospel effectively to people of all different times, places and customs. The obstacle of culture cannot make void the power of this Word.

6

Practical Tools for Bible Study

Any laborer needs good tools for his job. College students and lay people frequently ask about such tools. Which translation should I read? What concordances are available? These questions indicate that people are very serious about doing sound Bible study. Many people find it quite edifying and not at all difficult to learn enough Greek and Hebrew to make use of very valuable scholarly tools of interpretation. What follows are a few suggestions and aids for those seeking a deeper knowledge and understanding of Scripture.

Bible Translations
A question I hear frequently is, "What translations of the Bible should I use for my private study?" This is not easy to answer. There are so many excellent editions available that it is difficult to choose. Some differ from others only in matters of style and format and thus become a matter of literary preference for the reader.

Nonetheless, there are some basic and notable differences

between translations that ought to be recognized. These differences reflect different procedures and methods in preparing the translation. Of these differing methodologies there are three that are basic:

1. Verbal accuracy. The first method employed is that which seeks to follow the Greek (or Hebrew) text as closely as possible in a word-by-word pattern. Here strict fidelity to the ancient language is stressed in a verbal way. The strength of such a method is obviously found in its verbal accuracy. The weakness is its inevitable cumbersome and awkward literary style. To translate any document from one language to another in this manner makes for difficult reading. An example of this method of translation may be seen in the New American Standard Bible. Such translations are very useful for study purposes, but somewhat awkward for normal reading.

2. Concept accuracy. This method, which is the predominant method of modern translations, seeks a maximum of fluid reading style with a minimum of verbal distortion. Since words put together produce thoughts or concepts, the goal is to produce an accurate rendition of the thoughts or concepts of Scripture. Examples of this type may be seen in the Revised Standard Version and the New English Bible.

3. The paraphrase. The paraphrase method is an expansion of the concept method. Here the concept is extended and elaborated to insure that it is well communicated. There are various kinds of paraphrases. The J. B. Phillips "translations" exhibit the classic form of paraphrase. Ironically, Phillips himself did not consider his work paraphrase and was quite annoyed by this designation. But paraphrase it certainly was. A more recent phenomenon is the "modernized" paraphrase seen in such editions as the Living Bible and Good News for Modern Man. Here the premium is on readability and relevance to modern thought patterns. A radical experiment in such modernized paraphrase may be seen in Clarence Jordon's *Cotton Patch* version of the Bible. In this interesting effort biblical stories are retold in terms of modern culture.

The more a translation moves in the direction of paraphrase the more manifest is the danger of distortion. Though many paraphrases have been helpful introductions to Bible reading, they are not recommended for serious study. In my opinion, the weakest edition following this method is the Living Bible.

Annotated Bibles

Marginal notes and footnotes have been added to many editions of the Bible. In most cases, these notations are very helpful. Marginal definitions of archaic words, customs or articles can save the reader a trip to a Bible dictionary. The use of italics to note words added to the text by the translator is also helpful. Marginal notes indicating textual variants are likewise very important; textual variants indicate a discrepancy of the ancient texts which offer alternate reading. Following the science of textual criticism the translator must make a decision as to which of the alternate readings is to be used in translation. When the rejected alternatives are noted, it helps the reader become aware of that decision.

Cross-referencing is a common feature of many Bibles. Such devices make it possible to follow threads of thought throughout Scripture without constant reference to a concordance. Various methods of cross-referencing are available.

Commentary notes. Some editions of the Bible contain not only brief marginal notes such as mentioned above but provide a running commentary. The most famous example of this type of Bible is the Scofield Reference Bible and the New Scofield Reference Bible. I am personally opposed to such editions. My opposition is rooted not so much in the theological posture of the commentary but in the principle of running commentary itself. My main objection is based on the frailty of human memory. Time and time again I have seen people become upset when a speaker criticized an idea found in the notes of such Bibles: the listener was sure the speaker was criticizing the Bible itself. The problem is that a person opens his Bible and reads the printed page. Perhaps three-fourths of the print is the text of the Bible and the other fourth is the extended comment or note. Too often the average person fails to distinguish (especially later in recalling what was read) between the text of Scripture and the human comment. Because the comments appear on the same page as Scripture, this method tends to "baptize" these remarks in the minds of readers.

Some older editions of the Old Testament have printed on the first page of the Old Testament: "Genesis, The Book of Beginnings, 4004 B.C." No wonder countless people were ready to die for Ussher's speculative dating of creation at 4004 B.C.; they read it right in their Bibles! I want to emphasize, however, that the objection is one in principle and is not directed at one particular school of thought.

Translations and Commentary. In one sense every translation is a commentary: every translation involves the process of decision making with respect to words and ideas. Thus, a perfect translation will not be found. Even those translations produced by a check and balance system utilizing a team of scholars will inevitably reflect the individual or corporate bias of the translators. Such bias is frequently kept at a minimum and should not be cause of alarm. But the reader should be aware of this human frailty of translation.

By and large, the Jerusalem Bible is a superb translation, but on close examination it is not difficult to discern that it was produced by Roman Catholics. The Revised Standard Version deserves the widespread use it enjoys, but again, elements of liberal theology may be discerned within it. The New American Standard translation reveals its conservative bent. These are not reasons for wholesale rejection of such translations, but are words of caution that such tendencies not be overlooked.

The King James Bible

Any time a translation of the Bible enjoys the pre-eminent position of acceptance and usage over such a long period of time as the King James Bible has, there are bound to be howls of protest when its position of honor is threatened.

Some have charged that to replace the King James Bible is nothing less than the work of the devil! Others have acted as though the King James Version was a verbally inspired translation. It is not surprising to see such reaction. Because of its longevity, the King James Version has come to be precious to us as we hear its words echoed in literature, poetry, hymns and anthems. To hear the words of the psalmists, for example, in other translations sounds alien. What translation could possibly match the grand eloquence and majesty of language and style found in its pages? Hearing the King James Version read aloud is music to my ears. No one loves the beauty of this translation more than I.

But one fact concerning the King James Version cannot and must not be ignored: the King James Version is simply less accurate in its representation of the original writings of Scripture than most modern translations. There is a crucial historical reason for this. The Greek text from which the King James Version was translated (the *Textus Receptus*) is clearly inferior to more modern reconstructed Greek texts. Many textual errors found in the King James Version have been eliminated by more recent translations. Manuscript discoveries since the sixteenth century have greatly enriched our knowledge of the original texts.

Let one example illustrate the point: in the King James Version we read the following words in 1 John 5:7:

For there are three that bear record in heaven, the Father, the Word, and the Holy Ghost: and these three are one.

These words provide a clear and explicit reference to the Trinity. Such thrilling words should put an end forever to the Unitarian charge that the Bible doesn't teach the doctrine of the Trinity.

Now, I believe the Bible conveys, in a multitude of ways, the doctrine of the Trinity. I also believe the verse quoted above is a true statement. Yet, I am convinced that John did not pen those lines and they have no business appearing in the text of this Epistle. Why? Because the overwhelming testimony of our finest Greek manuscripts is against it.

These words do not occur in the earliest texts. If we can pinpoint the accidental inclusion in the biblical text of any scribal gloss, this is the one. These words, found in a fourth-century manuscript, were incorporated by Erasmus in his reconstruction of the Greek text in the sixteenth century. If we are looking for a beautiful translation, then the King James Version is the one. But, if we are interested in accuracy and purity of biblical translation, we must go beyond the King James Bible.

Commentaries

Commentaries are an indispensable tool for the student of the Bible. Without the use of competent commentaries I am abusing the principle of "private interpretation" by relying on my own judgment and my own judgment alone for understanding the Scriptures. Commentaries provide a check and balance to my own prejudicial tendencies.

Again, there are a wide variety of commentaries available to the ordinary reader. They range from single volume commentaries on the whole Bible to very technical works provided for individual books. They range from simple exposition to higher critical exegesis.

Single Volume Commentaries on the Whole Bible. The advantage of this kind of commentary is simply economics. A large volume of this type greatly reduces the cost of buying sets of commentaries. The disadvantage is their compactness and consequent brevity of comment. The comments are usually so brief that they cannot provide an in-depth analysis of the text. If you purchase such a volume, you would be wise to find one that has been put together by a team of scholars rather than by an individual. The reason for such a criterion is obvious. There is no one man who can write as good a commentary on the whole Bible as a commentary provided by men who have gained special expertise in individual books. My preference for whole Bible commentaries is *The New Bible Commentary* published by InterVarsity Press and Eerdmans.

Commentary Sets. Several sets of commentaries are

produced at different levels of scholarly depth. The more elementary commentaries include such series as The Cambridge Bible Commentary series, the Tyndale series and Barclay's Commentaries of the New Testament. Of these, I would not recommend Barclay. His commentaries have been very popular among laymen. They are eminently readable and spiced with excellent illustrative material. However, they betray a weak view of Scripture itself and tend to desupernaturalize the person and work of Christ. The miracles of the New Testament are often "explained away" and the message watered down.

More advanced series include the New International Commentary series, The Anchor Bible series, The International Critical Commentary series, and The Interpreters Bible. Of these, the most conservative is the New International Commentary series and the most liberal is The Interpreters Bible.

Individual Series. Much to be preferred to any series is the collection of commentaries written by individuals. This is by far the most expensive method of acquiring commentaries but also the most rewarding. Any series will contain strong volumes and weak ones. By being selective, one can acquire a more excellent collection. Dr. David Scholer has provided an excellent bibliography in this area: *A Basic Bibliographic Guide for New Testament Exegesis.* I strongly recommend this as a guide to selection of individual commentaries.

Concordances, Bible Dictionaries and Atlases
Every layman's "toolbox" should include at least one good concordance, one good Bible dictionary and one good atlas. The following concordances are excellent. The first three are based on the King James Version:
   R. Young, Analytical Concordance to the Bible
   J. Strong, The Exhaustive Concordance to the Bible
   A. Cruden, Complete Concordance to the Old and New Testaments
   M. C. Hazard, A Complete Concordance to the American

Standard Version of the Holy Bible
J. W. Ellison, Nelson's Complete Concordance of the
Revised Standard Version of the Bible
Bruce M. and Isobel M. Metzger, The Oxford Concise
Concordance to the Revised Standard Version of the
Holy Bible
The following are excellent Bible dictionaries:
J. Hastings, Dictionary of the Bible
G. Buttrick, The Interpreter's Dictionary of the Bible
F. C. Grant and H. H. Rowley, eds., New Revised Hasting's
Dictionary
J. D. Douglas, ed., The New Bible Dictionary
H. G. Gehman, ed., The Westminster Dictionary of the
Bible
The following are available atlases:
G. E. Wright and F. V. Filson, The Westminster Historical
Atlas to the Bible
L. H. Grollenberg (eds. Joyce Reid and H. H. Rowley),
Atlas of the Bible
C. F. Pfeiffer, Baker's Bible Atlas
H. G. May, ed., Oxford Bible Atlas

Foreign Translations
If you have a knowledge of one or more foreign languages,
you could put that knowledge to use in your Bible study.
Reading foreign translations of Scriptures can give subtle
nuances of meaning that may be better captured in a language other than English. Idiomatic renditions are particularly helpful. Many Americans have at least an introductory
knowledge of Latin. It is surprising to many people how even
a cursory knowledge of Latin can be used in Bible reading.
The Latin translations of the Bible tend to be very accurate.
One can see not only the relationship between the Greek and
Latin texts but the Latin roots of words that are brought over
into English.

Bible Reading Program for Beginners
Countless New Year's resolutions have been made and

broken in the Christian community regarding Bible reading. Promises to read the Bible from cover to cover are made and remade. Yet the fact remains that the vast majority of professing Christians have never read the whole Bible. Most have read the New Testament, but few have completed the Old Testament.

Why have Christians been so derelict when it comes to biblical study? Is it merely a lack of discipline or devotion? That may be part of the problem and consequently produces much guilt among Christians for leaving undone those things that should have been done. I think, however, that more than a problem of discipline, it is a problem of method.

We begin our Bible reading in a spirit of grim determination and diligently read the book of Genesis. Genesis provides important information about the foundations of biblical history and moves smoothly through the narrative history of the patriarchs. So far so good. Exodus is full of drama with the exploits of Moses and the liberation of Israel from the tyranny of the Egyptians. Cecil B. DeMille and Charlton Heston have given millions of us a sense of familiarity with these events. Then comes Leviticus. Here the attrition rate of interested readers begins to accelerate. Many of us who wade through Leviticus are finished off by Numbers. A few die-hards make it through Deuteronomy, and even a persevering few make it through the whole Old Testament.

Actually I have discovered that the majority of people who read the first five books of the Old Testament will make it through the whole Bible. Most people fail to read the Old Testament by getting bogged down in Leviticus and Numbers. The reasons are obvious. These books deal with detailed matters of the organization of Israel including lengthy lists of case law. So much of the material is foreign to us and makes difficult reading.

Yet, the information contained in these books is of crucial importance for understanding the scope of redemptive history. An accurate understanding of the New Testament depends on an understanding of these books. In fact, once a person acquires a general understanding of the whole scope of Scripture, he usually discovers that Leviticus and Numbers are fascinating and delightfully interesting. But without the general understanding the details seem somewhat unrelated.

To overcome the problems so many people have with reading the Bible I suggest an alternate route to our goal. Read the biblical books in the following order:

Genesis	*(History of Creation, Fall, and Covenant in Patriarchal history)*
Exodus	*(History of Israel's liberation and formation as people of God)*
Joshua	*(History of military conquest of promised land)*
Judges	*(History of transition from tribal federation to monarchy)*
1 Samuel	*(History of emerging monarchy with Samuel, Saul and David)*
2 Samuel	*(The reign of David, golden age of Israel)*
1 Kings	*(History of Solomon and the division of the kingdom)*
2 Kings	*(History of the fall of Israel and beginnings of the prophets)*
Ezra	*(History of the return from exile)*
Nehemiah	*(History of restoration of Jerusalem)*

Then read:

Amos and	
Hosea	*(Examples of Minor Prophets)*
Jeremiah	*(Example of Major Prophets)*
Ecclesiastes and	
Song of Solomon	*(Examples of Wisdom Literature)*
Psalms and	
Proverbs	*(Examples of Hebrew poetry)*

This list of readings gives an overview of the Old Testament and provides the framework for understanding it. It is the skeleton to which can be added the flesh and sinew of the other books after you have finished the New Testament skeleton. The following is the skeleton list for the New Testament:

Gospel of Luke (Life and teaching of Jesus)
Acts   (History of early Church)
Ephesians   (Introduction to teaching of Paul)
1 Corinthians   (Teaching in the life of the Church)
1 Peter   (Introduction to Peter)
1 Timothy   (Introduction to Pastoral Epistles)
Hebrews   (Theology of Christ)
Romans   (Paul's theology)

As with the Old Testament list, this gives us a basic familiarity with the component parts of the New Testament. After this is finished, we can go back and fill out the skeleton.

It is important to understand something of the dynamics of self-discipline. Self-discipline is easily acquired by first coming under the discipline of someone else. To complete this introductory program it would be wise to ask someone to supervise your reading program. If you can attend a class at church, it would be helpful.

What about Greek and Hebrew?

Americans tend to be somewhat intimidated by ancient languages, particularly Hebrew and Greek. One of the major fear-factors rests in the strange script used in these languages. Since we are unfamiliar with the unusual markings of Hebrew and Greek, it appears at first glance as "all Greek to us." Yet to gain a working knowledge of these languages for enriching our own Bible study is a relatively easy matter.

Let us look briefly at Greek as an example of improving our Bible study skills. Keep in mind that it is not necessary to have a complete knowledge of the Greek language to be able to use it for a specific task. We are concerned with acquiring an ability to work with one book. We are not preparing to work with the entire gamut of Greek literature. Thus, the task is greatly simplified and numerous tools have been already prepared to make the task even easier. The tools include the following:

1. Interlinear translations. An interlinear translation

provides the Greek text of the New Testament with the English translation given in parallel lines to the Greek. This gives the reader the opportunity to see at first glance how the Greek text is rendered into English.

2. *Metzger's frequency list.* Bruce Metzger of Princeton Theological Seminary has provided a labor of love for students of New Testament Greek. Certainly he is beloved of every seminary student who has had to face the task of studying New Testament Greek and was able to acquire this tool. Metzger's little booklet *Lexical Aids to New Testament Greek* can be acquired at virtually any seminary bookstore. It catalogues every word that occurs ten times or more in the New Testament, some 1,000 words in all. Thus, if a student works diligently for just a few weeks, he can easily master this list and have an excellent working knowledge of the vocabulary of the Greek New Testament. This tool reduces the task of learning vocabulary and is well worth the effort.

3. *Greek grammars.* There are many fine Greek grammar books that are available and would be quite suited for the ordinary reader. The most famous is J. G. Machen's *Introduction to the Greek New Testament.* Also helpful are the workbooks provided by James A. Walther of Pittsburgh Theological Seminary and W. S. LaSor of Fuller Theological Seminary.

4. *Greek lexicons.* Dictionaries of New Testament Greek can be used by anyone who learns the Greek script and alphabet, a task well worth the little effort required. The alphabet can be learned by a person with average intelligence in a few hours. If you know the alphabet, a whole new realm of tools, such as lexicons, are opened to you. The best standard lexicon is *A Greek-English Lexicon of the New Testament and other Early Christian Literature,* by W. F. Arndt and F. W. Gingrich. A less expensive and more brief lexicon is provided by G. Abbott-Smith, *A Manual Greek Lexicon of the New Testament.* As mentioned earlier, the most helpful tool of all which is open to anyone who knows the Greek alphabet, is Kittel's *Theological Dictionary of the New Testament.*

5. Other tools. Other language tools include analytical and topical concordances of the text of the Greek New Testament and of the Septuagint.

The same kind of aids and tools for Hebrew are also available. Hebrew helps include:

1. Frequency List. John D. W. Watts has compiled a list of commonly used Hebrew words under the title *Lists of Words Occurring Frequently in the Hebrew Bible.*

2. Hebrew Grammars. Among the Hebrew Grammar books available is Thomas O. Lambdin's *Introduction to Biblical Hebrew.*

3. Hebrew Lexicons. Lexicons available to the laymen include Brown, Driver and Briggs, *Hebrew and English Lexicon of the Old Testament.*

4. Hebrew Text. *Biblia Hebraica* by Rudolf Kittel is an example of Hebrew texts available.

The greater proficiency acquired in these tools the more enrichment is possible. It is a monstrous myth that such tools are only suited for the scholar. Scholars may be able to make more sophisticated use of them, but they are also beneficial for the layman. One need not be a professional carpenter to learn how to make good use of a hammer.

Conclusion

Modern historians are calling the twentieth century the post-Christian era. The influence of the church has been greatly eroded in our culture. That means the influence of Christian people has been weak. I believe that a crucial key for church renewal is to be found in adult education. I dream of a multitude of articulate and knowledgeable Christians making a new impact on our land. That dream cannot be realized unless we know and use the tools of intelligent Bible study. I hope that this book will serve as one tool to encourage that effort.

About the Author

R. C. Sproul, who is currently theologian-in-residence at Ligonier Valley Study Center, is widely known as a lecturer and author. He holds the bachelor of arts degree from Westminster College, the bachelor of divinity degree from Pittsburgh Theological Seminary and the doctors degree from the Free University of Amsterdam. He has served on the faculty of Westminster College, Gordon College, Gordon-Conwell Theological Seminary and Trinity Episcopal Seminary.

Among his publications are *The Symbol, The Psychology of Atheism, Discovering the Intimate Marriage* and *Objections Answered.* He also has contributed essays and articles in periodicals and collections of essays such as *God's Inerrant Word.* The present book marks his attempt to provide for interested laymen a basic approach to the science of biblical interpretation.

The Ligonier Valley Study Center which R. C. Sproul founded in 1971 is situated near Stahlstown, Pennsylvania and is dedicated to providing biblical and theological instruction to college students and other adults. The Center offers cassette tapes on many aspects of the Christian life and doctrine, as well as video tapes and a newsletter. The goal is to help Christians keep on growing in their knowledge of God and the practice of their faith. More information about the author and the Center is available from Ligonier Valley Study Center, Stahlstown, PA 15687.